Lionel Carley

London

September 1991

Coppard pp 31-47

BEGINNINGS

BEGINNINGS

by

ADRIAN ALINGTON

L. E. O. CHARLTON   A. E. COPPARD   A. J. CRONIN

E. M. DELAFIELD   LOUIS GOLDING

WYNDHAM LEWIS   V. S. PRITCHETT

V. SACKVILLE-WEST

BEATRICE KEAN SEYMOUR   HELEN SIMPSON

L. A. G. STRONG   ALEC WAUGH

MALACHI WHITAKER

THOMAS NELSON & SONS LTD

LONDON   EDINBURGH

PARIS   TORONTO   NEW YORK

First published, 1935

H. 81

CONTENTS

v

FOREWORD

THIS book has been compiled in the hope that it may have more than an entertainment value. To make it manageable, inclusion has been restricted to writers of fiction whose reputations belong to the post-war period. Even so, it is far from representative. Of the more obvious absentees, several were unable to contribute, and four unwilling. Each writer was simply asked to answer the question, "How did you begin?"

My own account appears, not because I think it particularly interesting, but because the publishers stipulated for it.

L. A. G. S.

BEGINNINGS

ADRIAN ALINGTON

IT is a curious and in many ways a heart-rending affliction, this mental restlessness which drives the most unlikely people to cover pages of virgin paper with words and sentences of their own devising, but those who are its victims know that there is no fighting against it. And indeed it has compensations: unpleasantnesses, even sorrows, may be transmuted by its means. I had a friend who, among other activities, wrote sensational stories for the cheaper magazines. He was often quite literally on the edge of starvation, but the odd fellow had only to begin tapping out on his decrepit typewriter such sentences as, " I sat in my expensively furnished room in the Albany, a cigar between my lips and a glass of rich old brandy at my elbow," to lose all sense of his own circumstances, and taste with quite astonishing reality the joys of high life. The thing goes even deeper than this, for those addicts who, like myself, are cowardly by nature, may almost forget to be afraid as the ship goes down beneath their feet, for the joy of note-taking during an unusual experience. Thoughts during a shipwreck. " If I survive," they think, " what a chapter this will make ! "

I must have suffered from the affliction at an early age, for I can remember, during my holidays from school, appointing myself editor of a magazine, to which the wretched members of my family were urged to contribute. Only one copy of each number was produced, and this I wrote out from beginning to end in my own hand, including the advertisements, editorial notices, and such juicy but unintelligible phrases as " All rights reserved," which gave a satisfactorily professional tang to the whole affair. I can remember composing for this magazine humorous articles, columns of jokes, a long narrative poem in blank verse after the style of the *Idylls of the King*, which we had read the term before at school, together with solemn descriptions in the fruitiest newspaper language of such events as local cricket matches, or the birth of a son to the gardener, or the winning by my mother of a croquet tournament. A very odd affair altogether.

The first paper in which I ever saw words of mine in print, as opposed to the neat and laboured handwriting of the holiday magazine, was *The Marlburian*. This was a few years before the war, when I was aged, I suppose, about sixteen. What my articles were about I cannot now remember, except that one was a sort of burlesque of a school story, but I have no doubt they were extreme rubbish. My house master, in any case, evidently thought so. He told me forcibly, and without any consideration for the feelings of an aspiring author, that my time would have been better employed in acquiring a higher place in form. In which there is no doubt that he was perfectly right.

The first efforts of mine to be received with any show of heartiness were both plays. The first, which was called *The Clue of the Bloodstained Spat*, was performed in the Upper School at Marlborough as the concluding part of a school concert, and photographs of it are still extant ; the second had its production nearly three years later in a large tent in the back area of the Somme battlefield during the winter of 1916. I have forgotten almost everything

3

about this contribution to the literature of the Great War, except its title, which was *What Every General Knows ; or, Sweet Fanny Adams*, and the fact that it was acclaimed with ardour by the troops. I do remember, however, the consternation of the performers on learning that the Brigadier had appeared and taken his place among the audience. For a while I, as the author of the piece, was unpopular with the company, but fortunately the General took its vigorous but rather crude satire on the Staff in excellent part. The evening passed off happily, after all; it is still sometimes spoken of at the annual battalion dinner, when memories are unlocked.

After these youthful excursions into the drama, I apparently came to the conclusion that Heaven had ordained me for a dramatist. During a brief incarnation as a post-war undergraduate, I was delivered of three or four one-act plays which met with varying fates. One was produced by Rosina Filippi, who was always a splendid friend to me, in Oxford; in it, I remember, the editor of the present volume, then an undergraduate, figured superbly as a tramp. Another, also originally done by Miss Filippi at her school in Chelsea, was afterwards

almost accepted by Lewis Casson for the Grand
Guignol ; a third was performed at a Charity
matinée at The Palace, and a fourth surprisingly banned by the Censor on the eve of its
performance as a curtain raiser. Very shortly
afterwards the ban was lifted, but by that time
the main piece was as dead as mutton, so that
this play was never performed.

Thereafter I seem still to have been obsessed
with the idea that I was born to be a play-
wright, for, quitting Oxford, I turned my back
rashly but resolutely upon security and the
ordered life, and determined to become an actor
with the idea of studying the conditions of the
stage at first hand. Accordingly I came to
London, settled myself in a combined room
off the Edgeware Road, and for some while
drifted humbly and obscurely about in theatrical
circles. J. B. Fagan was then running his
Shakespearian seasons at The Court, and I
became an inconspicuous member of his company. I marched with Falstaff's ragged army,
held a torch for Godfrey Tearle, who played
Othello (incidentally being set on fire one
evening by my fellow torch-bearer), and later
appeared in a different costume as a first, second,
or third gentleman. I forget which of the gentle-

5

men it was I enacted, but his part began with the words, " 'Tis one Iago, ancient to the general."

After that other similar engagements followed, including one with Martin Harvey in *The Only Way*. In this I was to have played one of the aristocrats who are haled off by numbers to the guillotine—once again I am vague about numbers, but it was the cowardly one—and I have a very distinct memory of Sir John patiently trying to teach me to utter a really blood-curdling scream into the emptiness of the Lyceum auditorium. First of all Sir John would emit a horrifying screech, and then I, in my modest way, would attempt to follow suit. It must have been a curious spectacle, the two of us standing there screeching at one another in the gloom of the empty theatre. But in the end my scream was a failure, and I never went to the guillotine. Instead I played other minor parts, and joined the crowd which roared and laughed at Sir John during his address to the tribunal—and what a lesson for any aspiring actor in sheer technical ability to put across an enormous speech ! But then Sir John is a grand actor, as any one knows who has seen him in plays like *The Burgomaster of Stilemonde*.

This was almost the end of my career as an

actor. Whether I really learned much about dramatic technique is doubtful, but certainly that mental notebook, without which those who are addicts of the strange vice I spoke of earlier can never travel, was a good deal fuller. In one respect a dressing-room full of small-part actors—particularly, perhaps, in those confused days just after the war—resembled a war-time mess ; it contained a richly varied assortment of human beings. Shakespeare, for some reason, seemed to attract the strangest of all. One dressing-room, for example, contained a former major in the Indian Army, an ex-schoolmaster who is now a leading musical critic, and a couple of old actors with a trail of dead dreams behind them.

Then in the same dressing-room there was X., that superbly erratic adventurer, who deserves a book of his own, and may one day get it, if I can ever bring myself to feel that I can do justice to X. Unlike the writing maniac, who carries his mental notebook everywhere, X. was the victim of another form of the same disease, for his life was a continuous melodrama, partly true, and partly of his own devising. To encounter X. was to pass immediately into a new and exciting world ; he had just received an offer to assist in the production of an obscene film which was to be made and smuggled abroad in a glorious atmosphere of closed motor cars, locked laboratories, and faked passports ; to enter a pub with him was to attract immediately the company of strange, flashy, or furtive men with stolen jewellery to dispose of ; while of his various matrimonial and amatory entanglements I cannot write here. X. always insisted that he was the younger son of a noble Irish family, who had been turned from home at an early age. How much truth there was in this farrago neither I nor any one else ever knew, but there is no doubt that X. himself believed and enjoyed it all. I met him again recently, and saw with dismay that he was grown fat and prosperous looking. But he had not lost his old touch. He was engaged, he told me, in the advertising profession, but he was evidently enjoying himself as much as ever, for while flying about the Continent in the pursuit of his business, he was being pursued by the police of several countries. I could not quite understand why, but with X.'s prosperous yet persistently ingenuous countenance before me, it would have been heartless to disbelieve.

There was Y., too, the ex-sailor, who, though less picturesque, was a ripe character. Y., who would grow pale with anger at the sight of a parson, because once one of that calling had run over his dog, and who was so little interested in the tragedy of *Othello*, in which we were both acting, that he had no idea at all of the course of the play after his own part in it was concluded. He was ignorant even as to whether it ended happily or not.

All this time, while I was failing to set the Thames on fire with my efforts as an actor, the itch to cover paper with words was not idle. And presently I figured as part author of a three-act play which was performed at The Everyman Theatre. In the sombrely sedate atmosphere, which at that time, at any rate, brooded over The Everyman, it withered, however, in a fortnight. I have always felt, too, that the actors were unnerved upon the first night by the conduct of an old gentleman in the front row of the stalls, who placed his goloshes on the stage. Subsequently altered and improved, the play was acted again at Portsmouth, with quite considerable success, but it never really recovered from the gloom of The Everyman (and the old gentleman's goloshes), and nothing came of it. But as I subsequently married the lady with whom I shared authorship (one of the very few entirely sensible and successful things that I have ever done), the affair may be said to have ended happily, so far as I was concerned at all events.

It was at this point of my life that I suddenly determined to become a novelist. Why I took this curious decision I cannot say. Why does anybody ever decide to become a novelist? In my own case, I suppose it was the old affliction at work, together with the feeling that I had acquired now a good deal of miscellaneous experience, which should not be wasted, but should be compressed into a single novel of outstanding merit. It was also now very necessary that I should make some money, and I thought—God forgive my innocence!—that to write a novel was a good way of doing it. At any rate, whatever my motives, I purchased a loose-leafed notebook and began.

Joseph Conrad, in *A Personal Record*, describes with a sort of gloating reminiscence, entirely characteristic of himself, the details of his initial day of authorship. He recalls how he rang for his breakfast to be cleared away. " I rang the bell violently, or perhaps I should

say resolutely, or perhaps I should say eagerly."
And presently the landlady's daughter appeared
" with her calm, pale face and an inquisitive
look." He recalls the weather precisely (" an
autumn day with an opaline atmosphere, a
veiled, semi-opaque, lustrous day with fiery
points and flashes of red sunlight on the roofs
and windows opposite,") and the smallest
details of his own sensations. All this makes
highly impressive reading. You are left with
a sense of profound issues at stake, of mo-
mentous things in the balance. You feel that
if the landlady's daughter, with her calm, pale
face, had failed to appear in answer to the
violent, resolute, or eager ring we should never
have had *Almayer's Folly*, or *Lord Jim*, or *The
Secret Agent*.

Anything of that kind, I'm afraid, is beyond
me. I cannot for the life of me remember
what the weather was like upon the day I
began my first novel, or the look of my landlady's daughter. But I do know that the book
itself grew laboriously in a number of different
places, in various bed-sitting rooms in London,
in a bungalow in Sussex, in a cheap hotel in
Paris, and part of it at least in the fascinating
half-Turkish little Jugo-Slavian town of Skoplje,

where a great friend of mine at that time figured as Vice-consul. I had planned to lay some of the scenes in the Balkans, and my friend, with whom I had travelled a good deal in former days, was helpful and enthusiastic. He went out of his way to bring me in touch with scenes and characters well fitted to my story. After undergoing many vicissitudes, my heroine became a dancer in a cabaret. And here my friend's assistance and social gifts were invaluable to me. We haunted the local cabaret, and amassed a great deal of information about the inside workings of this very arduous profession.

Not that it was always as simple as it sounds. One afternoon, I remember, in search of facts, we paid our respects to two ladies in their apartment, in a shabby quarter of the town.

" Now," said my friend, as our hostesses began to let loose a stream of highly technical terms, " get out your notebook."

It was unfortunate advice, for the ladies in question immediately conceived the idea that I was a detective, and became if not definitely hostile, at least suspicious and entirely dumb.

So in these varying parts of the world I laboured, and the novel grew. A customs official on the Jugo-Slavian frontier, examining my luggage, remarked in some bewilderment, " You certainly have much paper." And indeed this was no understatement. My novel reached gradually to enormous proportions. And as it grew I passed for the first time through the sensations which, I suppose, all those who set out to write a story pass through in their time. I knew those periods of elation which come when the characters take life and utter words, perform actions of their own, and the corresponding hours of discouragement when they remain obstinately creatures of sawdust, when the scene against which they are acting their parts seems tantalizingly to recede behind a mist. Most distressing of all, perhaps, were those times when I was convinced of the futility of all my efforts, oppressed with a sense of the world bustling, struggling, and suffering on all sides, and my own utter inadequacy to capture even the tiniest part of it all.

And my masterpiece grew and grew. There came, in due course, a time when I could labour no more, and the problem arose of getting it printed, published, and laid before a no doubt wildly appreciative public. Here I had a stroke of luck. Though I knew little or nothing of the inside of " the world of letters," it so happened that a man I had met in the course of the war—he had been Staff Captain at the Brigade Headquarters, at which I had for a while figured as a particularly inefficient Intelligence Officer—was now partner in a famous publishing firm. At the time of my Everyman Theatre venture he had written and invited me cordially to submit to him anything which might be suitable. Accordingly a day came when I shouldered the immense mass of paper which my novel had now become, and set off to beard my publisher friend in his office. That day I can remember with something like Conrad's clearness. I can remember fidgeting nervously about the waiting-room, staring at a pile of catalogues and shelves full of very clean books, and wondering—yes, I did, quite in the orthodox way—whether my own name would figure among them. I can remember, too, my publisher friend's kindness and tact. He displayed no signs of dismay at the ernormous parcel which I laid before him on the table of the waiting-room. He inquired the number of words which my masterpiece contained, and was unruffled at my reply. I retired, full of hope.

A short while afterwards I received a letter from my friend inviting me to go and see him. Still unfailingly courteous and polite, he explained to me that the thing was far too long.

" We might publish it at fifteen shillings," I can remember him saying, as though he had indeed contemplated such an enterprise, " but I cannot help feeling that in the case of an unknown author it would be a hazardous undertaking."

Was ever aspiring novelist more gently turned down ?

He suggested, first of all, that for my own satisfaction I should submit it to another publisher, and after that should set about reducing it to more reasonable proportions.

I took his advice in both particulars, dispatching it forthwith to a second publisher, who instantly rejected it. Here again I remember its return with a certain Conrad-like clearness. We were in the process of moving into a new flat. The great frost of February 1929 held London in its grip, strangling the water supply and defeating all our efforts to make the place habitable. I can remember sitting with my wife, each of us on a packing-case, regarding in despairing fashion the empty room, in which

15

it was not possible that we should ever live. As we sat there, facing one another in gloom, the caretaker appeared from below (no doubt with an inquisitive look on her calm, pale face) staggering beneath an enormous burden. And there was my load of paper again.

I saw then that my publisher friend was right, and without delay set to work to reduce my masterpiece. I set upon it, indeed, in a kind of frenzy. In the material world about me much happened. We moved at last into our new flat, and immediately the great frost relaxed its grip so that every pipe in the building burst. Water cascaded everywhere. Our new paint was ruined ; the house resounded all day long with the tramping feet and hoarse cries of plumbers. But all this was nothing to me. Sitting in a half-furnished room, the floor covered with books waiting to be put away and pictures to be hung, with the cries of the plumbers, who tried vainly to cope with the cascading streams of water, sounding outside, I hacked away in murderous fashion at my load of paper. I removed bodily whole paragraphs, even chapters ; I slaughtered characters with gusto. The mountain of paper decreased, and it was a salutary if somewhat humiliating

experience to find that as the result of my on-
slaught the novel was not only unharmed, but
actually improved.

When I had finished my task I again set off
to visit my publisher friend, again deposited
the now slightly less formidable mass upon his
waiting-room table. Again, after an interval,
I received a note asking me to visit him. This
time my friend invited me into an inner room.
We spoke of terms.

That day was the beginning of what to me,
at any rate, has been a very happy co-operation.
About once a year I appear at my friend's office,
bearing with me a new and, I trust, less un-
manageable parcel; with each new parcel I
receive, apart from the business aspect of the
case, much kindly and stimulating criticism.
Nor am I ever afraid of exhausting my friend's
patience, with any question whatever connected
with my work. Every author, I suppose, has
some one to whom he is indebted for a helping
hand at the beginning of his writing life. My
publisher friend has certainly been mine. And
whenever, as occasionally happens, people tell
me they have given birth to a novel, and ask
me what to do with it, my reply invariably is,
" Make a parcel of it and take it to Blank."

And so the business goes on, and once having embarked upon the practice of novel-writing it is difficult to stop, even if one were able to do so. I remember reading, not long ago, an article in *The Author* in which a well-known novelist, writing of his own output, compared himself to a certain box in a grocer's shop which he remembered from his youth. From this box there issued everlastingly a trickle of string ; however much the grocer chopped off, there was always a trickle of string left issuing from the box. The comparison seems to me so apt that I will borrow it, without apology.

I hope to continue producing novels until I die or become too decrepit to hold a pencil any longer. (At whatever age I finally arrive I shall never acquire the abominable habit of working on a typewriter ; can you not discern in many a modern story the harsh metallic sound of the keys rattling like dead bones ?)

Perhaps something of the first rapture goes, after a little while. Our third and fourth novel does not arouse us to quite the same pitch of excitement. But there are compensations. We come to realize that the periods of sterility which once seemed fatal, will pass ; we are no longer plunged into despair when we open little packets of press cuttings to find an unfavourable review (though my own modest experience has been that the leading reviewers err, if anything, upon the side of generosity, particularly in the case of new writers). The truth is, perhaps, that we come to realize how ephemeral are the works we produce—a few weeks of fairly vigorous life, if we are lucky, in bookshop and circulating library, and their little day is done. And if, perhaps, we carry in our hearts while we labour at our trade, the prayer that before we die a breath of something more than efficiency may creep into our work, and we may write something that was really worth writing— well, that is in the hands of the gods who watch over the whole curious business, and it is a thousand to one that we should be unaware of its coming. We can but labour and pray.

L. E. O. CHARLTON

ALTHOUGH his impersonal autobiography, published when he was fifty-two years old, happened to be Charlton's first considerable effort of authorship, it was by no means his earliest. The dame school at Coventry had been the scene of his first literary labours. Already prime favourite at the court of the headmistress, and fully conscious on that account of a growing disdain in the eyes of his mates, he found it necessary to consolidate the position. To that end he sought and received permission to establish a house organ, entitling it *The Radford House Chronicle*, and constituting himself proprietor, editor, and sole contributor. It was to be a monthly, illustrated with pen-and-ink sketches, and consisting mainly of a short story about school life, together with a special feature labelled " personalia," for which ample space had been reserved. The issue, produced in manuscript on lined foolscap, the most careful attention being paid to handwriting, was strictly limited to the one specimen copy.

The first two numbers were decidedly a success, and Charlton felt that he had scaled Parnassus. The columns devoted to " per- sonalia " were eagerly devoured, both by the headmistress and staff, who found therein the healthiest of outlooks on dame-school life; and by the boys as well, who consulted with each other as to the form which retribution should take. For the editor and sole contributor, feeling himself firmly entrenched, had not hesitated to pay off some old scores by filling the " personalia " space with a few well-directed personalities.

It was his undoing. Resentment flamed sky-high, and a dastardly plot was formed. The third number, then in course of preparation and only wanting the short story to make it com- plete, was filched from his locker and read aloud to an outraged community. Tears, protesta- tions, and, above all, a threat to inform au- thority, were alike unavailing. The offending number was consigned to the flames, burnt as if by the common hangman, and the mortally wounded author of the witty aspersions was dared to be a " tell-tale tit." Seventeen years elapsed before Charlton aspired again to literary fame.

His next attempt was the outcome of five years of service with the West African Frontier

Force in Ashanti and the Gold Coast hinterland. During that period, which immediately followed his return from the South African War, he had beguiled his leisure largely by learning the Hausa language, script and all, under the tutorship of one Ali Bagobiri, the regimental priest. He earned a substantial money reward as interpreter, and came in time to speak this West African *lingua franca* as well as any natives to whom it was not their racial speech. In addition, he made a collection of Hausa manuscripts, not easy in those early days to come by, which included proverbs, folk-lore, war-songs, and a few very fine religious poems.

Looking over the collection one day soon after he had left the Gold Coast for ever, he suddenly realized that here, under his hand, lay the material for a book, and he itched with a desire for authorship. The publishing house to which, in fear and trembling, he took the manuscripts was at once interested, and agreed to bring the book out provided he himself defrayed half the cost of publication.

This was far too good to be true, and he eagerly clinched the deal, plunging with terrific zest into the serious task of getting the material into shape. The whole West African adventure had thrilled him through and through. It had been the most colourful period of his life, and he longed for some means of setting a mark on the country so that he might not be the ordinary military wayfarer, attracted thither by a high rate of pay. There were no geographical laurels left to snatch, but the linguistic tree had hardly lost a leaf.

And so, in due course of time, *A Hausa Reading Book* was put forth by the Oxford University Press, and a clamouring public might possess it for the modest sum of four and sixpence, a third of which belonged to him for each copy sold. It was the year 1908 when the remarkable event occurred, but neither fame nor fortune came the way of Charlton. A small, ephemeral success the book did earn, making its expenses and a little more beyond. He had artfully arranged for its inclusion in a list of " books recommended," issued by the Colonial Office for the use of military and civil applicants for service on the West Coast, and a percentage of these had evidently felt a constraint to buy. But these sales soon fell away to nothing, and it became quite clear to the disappointed author that the efficient administration of Britain's Empire overseas was in no way dependent on any official knowledge of the language of the country. And yet the book would not die. The burst of health at birth had been succeeded by a lifelong invalidism, but still it lingered on. Although its heart-beats, measured by the sales return, grew ever feebler, the warehouse warmth in which it rested sufficed to sustain existence, bedridden as it lay. Only yesterday, twenty-six years since the date of publication, when the space it occupied was required for more urgent cases, was it mercifully pulped to death. *Requiescat in pace*.

After this attempt at authorship, twenty-three more years elapsed before Charlton tried again. But this time the circumstances were entirely different. He was fifty-two, seriously at odds with himself, and his next book wrote itself. The Air Ministry had just placed him on retired pay, and he was most concerned to discover a true reason for such a knock-down blow coming with harsh suddenness out of a fair sky.

As careers go his had not been unsuccessful, looked at from without. He was plentifully decorated, and had climbed up the ladder of promotion with unfaltering steps. Moreover, he had of late been entrusted, single-handed, with a technical survey of the Aircraft Industry,

24

which had employed him for three years on end of the closest application, and his submitted report had been acclaimed as a document of national importance. This was hardly the atmosphere for a forced retirement.

True enough, there had been one exceedingly black mark against his name. It was when, in Iraq, four years previously, he had tendered his resignation as Chief of Staff in protest against the policy of using Air Force units to bomb the desert tribesmen and the highlanders of Kurdistan. In doing so he had fully expected to bring his career to a sudden end, and had even marvelled when no such thing occurred. There had been stormy interviews instead, a period on half-pay, and a statement that he was not to expect further employment in a mandated territory. But that was all.

He had received a verbal promise, on the other hand, that the incident was over and done with for ever, and an appointment to command an area in the Midlands had been earnest of the undertaking. Promises did not possess terminal value like promissory notes, so his present plight as a late addition to the retired list could not possibly be related to the working of an ancient grudge.

It was all very puzzling. He was nursing no grievance. The notice in the London *Gazette* was as irrevocable as fate. It was the working of some natural law, and far too inveterate to allow place for petty resentment. The moment before, his star had shone as bright as Sirius; and now it was dead. The fault must lie within him.

In his quandary, Charlton turned to self-examination, not in the religious sense, *mea culpa, mea culpa, mea maxima culpa*, but for the purpose of trying to discover for himself what sort of person he really was, and why he had appraised his military talent at so much more than it was evidently worth. He would project his personality as on a screen, and write down exactly what he saw there, commencing at the dawn of memory and continuing until the present day. So he set himself to the task, and very soon found that he had discovered an occupation of absorbing personal interest.

Gradually the original motive receded into the background, though it was always inherent in the design, and he gave himself up completely to the delights of literary creation. To realize at the end of an episode, or after an account of reaction to circumstance, that he had expressed himself with exactitude, and

26

that as composition it was not too bad, pleased him beyond measure. He determined to finish the " life " whatever betide, and to present it in manuscript to the head of the family, to be read by descendants fifty or a hundred years hence. No thought of publication had then crossed his mind.

Very early in the day he had found difficulty in handling with elegance the constantly recurring " I." It seemed impossible to avoid egoism on the one hand, and on the other not to feel too naked and unprotected when the more delicate and intimately personal recollections were under consideration. He felt that the work, for whatever it was worth, must inevitably suffer in the standard of ruthless candour he had determined on, unless some alternative style could be found. And then he bethought him of *The Education of Henry Adams*, and of the remarkable exposition of character in it as a result of using the third person instead of the first.

It was a book he had always immensely admired, and he promptly read it again. At once the way was open, and this would be his model. He commenced afresh, to find the former difficulty no longer there. The thin veil of anonymity thus bestowed served the exact purpose of allowing him to reveal himself without the sense of shame, to be personal and sincere without crude egoism, and to offer comment without the feeling of conceit.

He showed the work in progress to a sister, to a brother, and was heartened by their criticisms. He showed it to a great friend, who was also a writer of high repute, and he heartily commended it. It was then that Charlton felt once more the itch to be an author. He argued thus. He was not a distinguished person in any way, and there was therefore no real reason why people should want to read about him. At the same time he had had a varied career, spotted with incident and adventure, and, anyhow, a human document, strictly informed as this one would be with the purpose of truth, could not fail to bear an appeal to that section of the reading public inclined to such literature. But it must be well written and told, with humour and with an impress of utter sincerity. In that way it might get over, and might even be helpful to a few who would possibly see themselves in Charlton's distorted mirror. He would have a shot at it.

When the book was wearily approaching a conclusion, he sought an introduction to a literary man of eminence, and produced a few of the earlier chapters for advice and criticism. The result exceeded all expectation. The great man not only said that it would do, he said that it would do indeed, and then and there he went on to guarantee publication.

In this way *Charlton* in due course appeared, under the imprint of Faber and Faber. He was at last a real author, and could flatten his nose against booksellers' windows with a fair certainty of seeing his own stupendous work on sale within. Those were proud moments, even though they lasted for only a short season. In the course of his search for self he had discovered a small writing ability. For whatever reason he had been retired from active life in his Service he was glad of it now, and rosy vistas of a literary future opened up before him. He had tasted blood.

He had tasted also of the joy which even a small quantity of money can give when earned directly by the sweat of the brain, the publisher's cheque having put this flavour in his mouth, and Mr. Frank Morley suggested to him that he might try his hand at a book of adventure for boys. It was like playing chess without a queen, said Mr. Morley. This appealed mightily to the budding author, who had hitherto preferred, in his own game of life, to dispense with the more hide-bound formalities, and he lustily set to work.

He produced two books of the sort in fairly quick succession. Plenty of material was to hand, for he had experienced a good deal in many different places, most of them the natural scenes for exciting events. He rummaged in memory for forest and desert impressions, and the way of life therein. Island life in Atlantic and Pacific was vividly recalled, and also garrison reminiscences in India and the Mediterranean. It was as if he were ransacking a curio cupboard, long forgotten in an attic, and finding most unexpectedly that these oddities, acquired without effort in the course of time, did actually possess an interest for the sort of boy which he had once been. And so to his first novel, *The Stolen Expedition*, which was published by Nelson, and greeted by the reviewers with a favour which surprised him.

He thinks he will go on doing this sort of thing for ever. He will not take root and let the years go by until the next one is the last. The future lies ahead, but the past, with a double significance for him, is behind.

A. E. COPPARD

WHATEVER else may be the outcome of this little essay, I do not think it will reveal any peculiar secrets—if such things exist—of the art of writing fiction. And were I in possession of them, I would not boggle at their disclosure, for it is clearly vain for any one who has not a natural gift for telling a tale, of whatever order, to seek some royal road to the public fancy; while those who have that natural tendency will go their own regardless road, unconscious of a secret or any rules and principles.

And as to this mysterious desideratum, this natural tendency, there is a warning to be given : do not mistake an intense desire to do a certain thing as being in any way indicative of a natural talent for its performance. All my life I have harboured a passion to excel at speech-making, at singing, at playing football, but after years of instruction I am still unable to make a reasonably good shot at any of these things. Moreover, it seems to be taken for granted that a facility with the pen—particularly when it derives from Oxford or Cambridge—is an indication of talent, that a person thus gifted has only to sit down and transcribe his impression of a thing for a work of art to spring like a grasshopper from the page.

How illogical !

No one imagines that a boy who can hammer a nail into a plank is, *ipso facto*, capable of constructing a piano case; that a man who plays billiards is necessarily qualified to build the table he plays on; or that a person who can sing his tonic sol-fa is a Schubert in the making; yet there are thousands of persons who, on no more evidence than the composition of tantalizing letters to exasperating tradesmen, deem themselves competent to write novels. What is more, they proceed to write them; what is worse, they sometimes get them published.

A fallacy at the other end of the scale is the notion that art is the outcome of something which is called inspiration, a divine effluent or an epilepsy, which, seizing the unconscious medium, belches forth *Pickwick*, *Anna Karenina*, *The Song of Solomon*, and *Heartbreak House*. There is no such thing. It is true I am not the author of any of those works, but speaking in all humility for myself, I repeat there is no such thing. There are days when the faculties are on their best and liveliest behaviour, permitting the amplest easiest flow, what George Moore calls " halcyon days of fifteen hundred, two thousand, sometimes two thousand five hundred, words in the day," but such occasions are generally governed by a flowering of natural conditions. Given the talent, they will recur to the writer as constantly as a century recurs to Bradman. In my youth I was a bit of an athlete, also I was fond of playing billiards. I noticed I played billiards best, not so much after I had been practising a lot upon the tables as when I had been training a lot upon the track—that is to say, when I was physically fit.

Now although the art of writing fiction cannot be taught, it would be folly to deny that it can be developed by study and experiment ; but that study and experiment must certainly be undertaken by *yourself*, on your *own* terms : it must not be sought for at the hands of any other authority. Indeed, any desire for instruction to be imposed on you from without is itself a denial of your natural genius and fitness to be

an author at all. Authors are born, not made,
and if you cannot develop your genius yourself
it is unlikely that anybody else can do it for
you.

" The story teller comes into the world fully
equipped almost from the first, finding stories
wherever he goes as instinctively as a reaper in
the cornfield discovers melodies that the professor of counterpoint and harmony strives after
vainly in his university."

That was George Moore's belief—at least,
it is what he said—so you see that right from
the beginning you must be in possession of
what I call the Fictional Mind, that is to say
a mind that goes about noting people and
events and conversations for the sinister purpose
it has in view ; a mind that, when it meets a
stimulating occasion, begins to effervesce and
bubble over in extra-truthful amplifications ;
a mind that is constantly conspiring and conceiving plots, or bits of plots, modifying or
extending them as it thinks fit ; in short, the
mind of a liar, who desires to supplement truth
in the interests of romance. Perhaps, on some
very rich occasion, we may call it a mind that
supplements a fact or an idea, and thereby
produces an image of beauty.

34

As a boy, although my father had bought me the plays of Shakespeare before I was nine, I much preferred to nourish my fancy with stories about Deadwood Dick, Calamity Jane, and such like " bloods." As a youth I became terribly mixed up with athletics and poetry, although I cannot trace either of these phases to Dickens, who had by then become a god of mine. At twenty-one I was a young man mad about poetry. Monstrous—it seems to me now, though it did not then—to have combined this mania with the training of pugilists and runners, and the sale of soap ! But so it was. In the public library at Brighton I read the whole of Johnson's Poets in some thirty or forty little brown duodecimos (how I loved Hudibras Butler and Abraham Cowley !), and I acquired a Chaucer as a selected prize in a literary competition, together with a *Paradise Lost*, which I bought for twopence — printed at The Two Bibles in Essex Street, 1724. It must have been somewhere about then that I submitted an awful poem of mine to *The Yellow Book*, not knowing that the periodical had been defunct for several months !

What gave my mind its real set towards prose writing was the reading of Thomas Hardy's short stories. In them for the first time I found what I had longed for in a contemporary book, recognized the moment I opened *Life's Little Ironies*—poetry in prose ; the element that had so enamoured me in that great tale of Noah and the Flood, and was to enrapture me again years later when the Constance Garnett Tchechovs' began their enrichment of English literature. Of course I do not mean prose poetry or any capricious flights in the use of words ; I mean that rare and poetic spirit transcribing its lovely apprehensions as though specially for me, for me alone—my heart leaped up at the undying vision.

But this is not to be an autobiography ; I have to tell you how I began.

Somehow I seem to have forgotten much of that, but I do remember how, from that time onwards, I read short stories with a view to writing some myself—some day, very much later on—when I should feel inclined to do so. I had no particular " call " to write anything except poetry, and I didn't write much of that— it was so infernally difficult. For you cannot steep yourself in the Masters without acquiring a standard of your own, and my standard rose eagle-high month by month, far beyond the reach of my wren's capacity. But there, what is the use of an ideal if it does not exceed your grasp ? What happened, then, was that I went to work at an iron foundry in Oxford, and by some fortunate chances I met in that city a number of undergraduates who were students of literature. Since then many of them have become famous. At that time most of them were only half my age, but they showed me poems and stories they had written ! I had not written a single passable line. I was always going to, mind you. Oh, yes ! Tucked away in some dulling corner of my head was the notion that I would begin something soon—all in good time !—and now, here were all these boys with their poems and tales already written, some of them even in periodicals, and one or two in real proper books ! Straightway I was fired, though not by any more worthy muse than the spirit of emulation. My competitive humour was aroused ; it was time I, too, had a go, although I was starting from scratch. I started. Some wise instinct had led me, years before, to jot down in notebooks all my observations, impressions, thoughts, and plots. This has become a habit which I indulge to this day. These notes, accumulated through the years, provided me with a mass of material, though much of it was useless.

A small nephew of mine once asked me this riddle : Why is an author the queerest animal in the world ? Because his tale comes out of his head ! The answer is good enough for a riddle, but it is not good as an explanation. The tale does not really, or not very often, come *out* of the author's head — it merely comes *through* it. You may want to make a box for some domestic purpose ; you know all about the making of boxes, you have the necessary tools—the saw, the hammer, the pincers, plane, and nails—but you cannot make the box until you have procured some timber to make it with. The imagination cannot feed upon itself. No matter how finely equipped your imagination may be, you cannot exercise it until you have something to exercise it upon. That something the true story-teller will always find in the common matters of the world that lie around him. But ordinary life is no more interesting than ordinary business, so in fiction ordinary life will have to be transmuted : that is to say it will have to be presented in a way that heightens and magnifies its unperceived significancies. There is no life that is important or significant as a whole, not even the greatest ; therefore the fiction-monger must always be more or less untruthful. He has to persuade you that his fanciful view of a certain process or event is a precise and real one. What is important in art is not truth itself, but the sensation of truth. Adventures in fiction are distilled and heightened and crowded in a way impossible to mere life. In an hour we may read the history of a human soul, and thenceforward something in ourselves is definitely changed.

By this process the budding author—if he has a first-class mind, and only then—may achieve some first-class results, often in spite of inadequate material. If he hasn't got a first-class mind there will always be plenty of first-class critics to tell him so, though they seem powerless to instruct him. Possibly they may give him some advice, almost certainly he will receive a label diagnosing his work as subjective, objective, romantic, realistic, rural, cosmopolitan, highbrow, or lowbrow. There are indeed scores of these quaint categories into many of which he will be planted by as many different assessors, and for any subsequent trespass from them he may quite easily be

wolfed by Humbert, or be gored by Gould.
These labels are perplexing. One might in all
simplicity take realism, for instance, to mean
that a story conceiving a whole year's life of
any man should take exactly a year to write and
exactly a year to read. If it does not do that,
you may possibly think your writer is being
merely romantical ; but he is not—he is being
helplessly untruthful, a lowbrow in fact. And
so on. I have never read any notices of my
own books that gave me the slightest assistance
in learning the craft of story-telling. I learned,
it is true, that tastes differ, that while certain
things in my tales gave displeasure, other
things gave enjoyment ; but this did not tell
me how to write. It only showed me that in
order to please somebody whom I did not
know I should have to suppress phases of
myself which at least gave *me* great pleasure.
I would not for a moment deny the public's
right to be gratified ; indeed, the author who
writes without his eye on the approbation of his
readers is very imperfectly equipped—why on
earth should he publish at all unless his final
goal is acceptance by the public ? But no
writer ever gained much by cutting off his right
hand and transferring the pen to his left.

But this story of how I began contrives to slip away, leaving me speculating on how *you* would fare were *you* ever engaged on the like adventure. Let me get back to my bundle of fiction material, the notes I had accumulated.

I found I had seldom got hold of a plot in its entirety ; it was generally no more than an episode, or a piece of a plot, just patches and fragments that seemed to promise something. My job was simply to sit down with these fragments and devise a framework for their proper use. And what was their proper use ? Their proper use was merely something I had to tell, which I thought had not been told before, and which I wanted to tell in my own way. There were imaginary predicaments I wanted to solve, and I had to find imaginary people to solve them for me. A novelist may very well conceive the outline of a character, and, working from that character, devise a sequence of events to bring out his magical view of him ; but a short story writer must reverse this process, must first catch his plot and then devise characters to fit it. In a way he is something like a detective who has been given one or two clues and told, not to discover any criminal or solve any mystery, but to interpret some problem which is embodied in these vague elements. Here again I cannot tell you how it is actually done! There is no formula. Each problem is very different—some are easy, some hard, and most of them so bulging with issues which it would be unwise to enlarge upon that it becomes mainly a question of elimination. It would take too many pages to show in any detail how I worked, and the broad questions of construction, of angles of approach, as well as of the general technique of writing, are so magnificently illuminated in the prefaces which Henry James wrote for the collected edition of his books that I need do no more than direct you straightway to the same fountain of suggestion of which I made use. The peculiar virtues of elimination which I studied to acquire are effectively illustrated in the great tale of Noah and the Flood.

The tale begins with the announcement that the earth was corrupt, and God therefore was about to destroy mankind. There is neither description nor explanation of the world's wickedness, you just take it for granted, it is unimportant. Noah is commanded to make the ark, and as the ark is the great thing in the

story, we are given some lovely details of its
construction—its length, its breadth, its height.
It is to be made of gopher wood, pitched within
and without with pitch, to have three storeys,
lots of rooms, and *a* window and *a* door.   Then
Noah is told who to admit into the ark—his
human family and the other living creatures.
Noah does all this in seven or eight verses, and
moves into the ark.   And then what does the
story tell you ?   It proceeds to tell you how *old*
Noah was, tells you the day of the month—the
seventeenth day of the second month of Noah's
six hundredth year.   Then it tells you it rained
for forty days and forty nights, that the flood
covered the mountain-tops, and that every
living thing without the ark was destroyed.
But God remembered Noah, and after a hundred and fifty days of this colossal catastrophe,
naïvely described in precisely one hundred and
ninety words (a little more than one word per
day !), the ark came to rest on the mountains
of Ararat, and the author, realizing that it is
about time to get some precision into this part
of the narrative, gives you the exact date of the
ark's arrival there : it was the seventeenth day
of the seventh month.   On the first day of the
tenth month things were getting better, and

forty days later Noah opened the window and sent forth first a raven and then a dove.

" And he sent forth a raven, which went forth to and fro, until the waters were dried up from off the earth.

" Also he sent forth a dove from him, to see if the waters were abated from off the face of the ground ;

" But the dove found no rest for the sole of her foot, and she returned unto him into the ark, for the waters were on the face of the whole earth : then he put forth his hand, and took her, and pulled her in unto him into the ark.

" And he stayed yet another seven days ; and again he sent forth the dove out of the ark ;

" And the dove came in to him in the evening ; and lo, in her mouth was an olive leaf pluckt off : so Noah knew that the waters were abated from off the earth.

" And he stayed yet other seven days ; and sent forth the dove ; which returned not again unto him any more."

On New Year's Day the face of the earth was dry. On the twenty-seventh of the second month Noah left the ark. He then sacrificed an offering to the Lord. And of what did this offering consist ? It consisted mainly of his fellow-travellers, just one of every clean beast and fowl that had come through alive. (Noah ! Noah !)

This magnificent and wonderful yarn is folk tale at its best. There are other versions of The Deluge, probably enshrining some memory of an actual catastrophe. What the tale-teller had to do was to explain how, if the whole earth was covered with water, anything survived at all. That was his problem, so he doesn't waste any time in describing the wickedness of the world ; you are not plagued with any of the immense issues, such as how mankind died, or what the last man said to Noah, or he to him, but you are given much detail about the building of the ark with its one window and a door. No definition of clean and unclean beast, but just a record of seven and seven, or two and two, as the case might be. No account of the infinite labour of assembling couples of every beast, bird, and serpent from the tropics to the poles—only that they " went in." No reference to what happened throughout that long voyage of a year ; and as for the flood, well, it rained for forty days and forty nights until the mountain-tops were covered. What more do you want ? After such shameless avoidance of every indubitable difficulty comes that miracle of a gesture, when Noah opened the window and sent forth the raven and the dove ; it is full of minute detail, down to the single leaf of a tree, even to Noah putting his hand out of the window.

As an example of the art of elimination flawlessly carried out, this tale is supreme. I am sure that a modern writer would make the greatest use of the very material here so calmly put aside. He would certainly let himself " go " at that storm and the inundation. Victor Hugo, in *The Toilers of the Sea*, describes a storm which you think never *will* come to an end—there are pages, and pages, and pages of it. The ark goes floating about on the face of the waters ; what was happening inside it ? Our writers would surely make that the cream of the narration, but in this tale you have four prominent features : the ark, the animals, the flood, and the bird. For a modern writer the prominent features would be : the world's wickedness, the storm, and what happened inside the ark during its mighty journey. And, of course, it would have to be a novel, probably a trilogy—possibly even a " saga."

It was upon some such training as this that

I began to handle my material while still clerking at Oxford. I wrote some tales. I wrote them very slowly, with infinite pains, spending delightful weeks upon their revision. " Oh, my countrymen," says Sterne, " be nice ; be cautious of your language ; and never, oh, never let it be forgotten upon what small particles your eloquence and your fame depend." I accumulated about a dozen of these tales. I showed them to my friends. They liked them, they seemed to think they were good. Meanwhile my poetry had begun to improve, and some pieces appeared in journals like the *Nation* and the *Westminster Gazette*, so one day I sent off all my dozen tales, each to a different editor. Only one was accepted. It was a tale called " Piffingcap," which *Pearson's Magazine* (to my dismay !) printed in a special holiday number " edited by George Robey." Later in the same year (1918) the *English Review*, under Austin Harrison, printed one called " Dusky Ruth," while others were taken by the *Manchester Guardian* and the *Westminster Gazette*. I concluded all was well with me, and so, the war being over, I gave up my job on All Fools' Day 1919. I was forty-one—it was now or never !

A. J. CRONIN

THE record of my beginning ought really to be entitled, "How Not to Become an Author." I do not submit it as an exemplar, but rather as a Warning. (Yet I *am* apparently an author, and, to my amazement, an author who makes a living from his trade.)

Most novelists who suddenly blaze into print after they have reached the thirties have practised their vice secretly for years. If you tax them with it they may pass the thing off with a laugh, but in their hearts they cannot remember a time when they did not long to write. (Arnold Bennett, for example, is reputed to have composed a sonnet at his mother's knee ; while Ethel Mannin produced some scintillating essays before the age of puberty.) But I . . . I concealed no demiurge beneath my childish jersey. And in my adult life, for fifteen weary years, I wrote nothing but prescriptions.

Often, I admit, there were moments during

my work as a doctor when the peculiarity of some patient would move me to that inhuman delight in the oddness of life which is one of the basic elements of the novelist's attitude. I did feel that here was something of life, something vivid and vital which deserved to be set down. But at the end of the consultation, when the pen went to paper, it was only to record : Rx. The mixture as before.

Many people, by-the-bye, contemplating the number of doctors who have become novelists— Conan Doyle, Georges Duhamel, Somerset Maugham, Helen Ashton, de Vere Stacpoole, and Warwick Deeping, are names which come immediately to mind—must have wondered whether there is not some important point of liaison between these two professions. But if in my own case some connection must be found, it was merely that the rigours of general practice led me to long (naïvely, as I now know to my cost) for the " quiet haven " of authorship. And so once or twice during my medical years, after a particularly trying day, the notion of a novel would enter my head, and I would remark speculatively to my wife : " You know, I believe I could write a bit if I had time."

And she, looking at me over her knitting,

49

would reply kindly: " Do you, dear ? " Then, very tactfully, lead me to talk about my golf handicap.

But for Nemesis—or, in humbler language, a piece of seemingly bad luck—I should probably still be dealing out bromides to neurotic spinsters. There is said to be a destiny which affects our ends. In my case it affected my inside. After I had been practising several years in the West End of London, I developed what, in the army, used to be summarily denoted as a " gastric stomach." I was, so to speak, hoist with my own petard : for ten years I had been handing out all sorts of delightful complaints, but now some of my friends in Harley Street put their heads together and handed out this one to me. I protested. I think I said that their action amounted to a breach of medical etiquette, but it was no use. The sentence, in the traditional Harley Street manner, was immutable : low diet and six months' rest without the option.

And then, as I got up from the couch in that wretched consulting room and began to hitch my braces, a dazzling thought transfixed me.

" By heaven ! " I thought, " gastric stomach or no gastric stomach, now I have the opportunity to write a novel." And on my way home, remembering that spelling had never been my strong point, I stopped at Mudie's and bought an English dictionary.

And so, symbolically at least, with the dictionary in one hand and a tin of Benger's in the other, I set out for the Western Highlands to create a masterpiece. Strictly speaking, then, my first book, *Hatter's Castle*, was the product of a disordered digestion and not, as one lady who wrote to me inferred, of a disordered mind.

I ought here to say that my family had accompanied me to the farm outside Inveraray —a place chosen with much care as being suitable for the birthplace of a Great Work—and now they awaited developments with interest.

You see, having emphatically declared before my entire household that I *would* write a novel (tacitly inferring, of course, that it was the fault of every member of this household that I had not already written twenty novels), I found myself faced with the unpleasant necessity of justifying my rash remarks. All I could do was to retire, with a show of courage and deep purpose, to the little room upstairs which had been at once selected as " the room for Daddy to write in." Here I was confronted by a square deal table, which my wife insisted was " just the thing," by a neat pile of virgin two-penny exercise books, and—precisely laid out beside the books—by the English dictionary I had purchased so sanguinely. Nor must I forget the Benger's, treasured in some suitable domestic background, for I am proud of that bland stimulus. Too often in the bad old days brandy has been the chief inspiration of long-winded novelists.

It was the morning following our arrival. Amazingly—for that latitude—the sun shone. Our little rowing boat danced entrancingly at anchor on the loch, waiting to be rowed. My car stood in the garage, waiting to be driven. The trout in the burn lay head to tail, waiting to be caught. The hills stood fresh and green, waiting to be climbed. And I—I stood at the window of the little upstairs room. I looked at the sun, the loch, the boat, the car, the burn, and the mountains ; then sadly turned and sat down before my deal table, my exercise books, and my dictionary. " What a fool you are," I said to myself gloomily, and I used an adjective to magnify my imbecility. How often during the next three months was I to repeat that assertion—each time with stronger adjectives.

But in the meantime I was going to begin. Firmly I opened the first exercise book, firmly I jogged my fountain pen out of its habitual inertia. Firmly I poised that pen and lifted my head for inspiration.

It was a pleasant view through that narrow window : a long green field ran down to a bay of the loch. There was movement. Six cows, couched in the shadow of a hawthorn hedge, ruminated ; an old goat with an arresting beard tinkled his bell in search, I thought, of dandelions ; a yellow butterfly hovered indecisively above a scarlet spurt of fuchsia ; some white hens pottered about, liable to sudden flusters and retreats, some more majestic fowls strutted in sudden excitements and pursuits.

It had all a seductive, dreamlike interest. I thought I might contemplate the scene for a minute or two before settling down to work. I contemplated. Then somebody knocked at the door and said, " Lunch time." I started, and searched hopefully for my glorious beginning, only to find that the exercise book still retained its blank virginity.

I rose and went downstairs, and as I descended those white scrubbed wooden steps, I asked myself angrily if I were not a humbug.

Was I like the wretched poet d'Argenton in Daudet's *Jack*, with his Parva Domus, Magna Quies, and his *Daughter of Faust*, which, as the days slipped on, never progressed beyond that still-born opening sentence : " In a remote valley of the Pyrenees teeming with legends " ? Was I like that ? I carved the mutton glumly. My two young sons, removed by their nurse to a remote distance in order that they might on no account disturb the novelist, had returned in spirits. The younger, aged four, now lisped breezily : " Finished your book yet, Daddy ? " The elder, always of a corrective tendency, affirmed with the superior wisdom of his two additional years : " Don't be silly. Daddy's only half finished." Whereupon their mother smiled upon them reprovingly : " No, dears, Daddy can only have written a chapter or two."

I felt not like a humbug, but like a criminal. For my worry was not merely the ridiculous one of justifying myself before the household, but a far greater anxiety about our future. Naturally this enforced rest would eat into my savings, and the prospect of ultimately returning to a profession I disliked would not hasten my recovery. It seemed to me that the success of this projected novel was my only hope. And yet I had wasted a whole morning dreaming at a window !

I remembered the aphorism of an old schoolmaster of mine. " Get it down," he used to declare. " If it stays in your head, it'll never be anything. Get it down." So after lunch I went straight upstairs and began to get my ideas down.

I took immense pains with that first chapter, and laboured over such redundant details as a minute description of the " Castle," reading up Architecture in the Encyclopædia in my burning desire for accuracy. I can smile now at the many hours I spent creating this and other waste tissue. But then, some of the technical difficulties of writing proved very great. For instance, I was always dissatisfied with the construction of sentences, and went to endless trouble to alter them into forms far less effective than the original. Again, I wrote the first two parts without in the least knowing what was going to happen in the third book, but here the character of the Hatter came to my aid and carried the novel to its inevitable ending.

Indeed, I could fill a volume with the emotional experiences of those next three months. There were, inevitably, moments when the

thing possessed me, and I thought—surely,
yes, surely this is worth while. You remember
how Thackeray, writing feverishly far into the
small hours of the morning, finished that scene
in *Vanity Fair* where Becky is discovered by
her husband, Rawdon, with my Lord Steyne,
and how, carried away by his own feelings,
Thackeray threw down his pen and cried to the
empty room : " Sublime, sir ! By heavens,
it's sublime ! "

Blundering along in this first incoherent
attempt at self-expression, it came even to me—
a faint gleam of this achievement, the feeling
that something was rising out of the dead
words.

But there were other moments—not moments, but hours, and even days—when nothing
in the universe was right, when I classed myself
morosely as an inept, presumptuous fool—
madder than the Hatter I was attempting to
create. I shall never cease to wonder how I
managed to finish this first novel. I had no
reason whatever to believe that I could succeed
in the task I had set myself. But my lack of
confidence was balanced by the ceaseless drive
of my anxiety. I argued with myself that
failure meant a return to doctoring, that I

must carry through this one attempt to escape. If it was unsuccessful I could at least return to my work and resign myself to my fate knowing that I had made the only possible effort for freedom. However, in spite of my reasonable arguments, these alternating moods were difficult to subdue.

I remember vividly the day—it was in point of fact my birthday—when the typescript of Book I. arrived from London. My typist, an elderly, infirm lady who had been a patient of mine, had done her work nobly. Yet, when I read those first chapters, my heart sank within me. " Have I," I asked myself, " written this awful, this incredibly awful nonsense ? " The words leapt at me from the pages with devastating banality. I felt not like an author but like an idiot, and I had the impulse there and then to tear up all that I had written, to abandon the whole thing. Without knowing it, I had reached that stage which, I am now informed, every author reaches with every book. It is the stage when the author stands, so to speak, with his manuscript in his hand and cries out to the moon : " Am I going on with this, or am I not ? " This rather touching picture of an author at the cross-roads is faintly reminiscent of Alice's interview with the Cheshire Cat. But the position, though ludicrous, is not altogether pleasant, and the impulse towards destruction—I mean, naturally, of the manuscript—is a powerful one.

In my own case, for better or worse, I withstood temptation—the balance fell against the tearing. I went on writing. I wrote harder than ever. I wrote, indeed, as many as five thousand words each day. I finished the book with a last desperate spurt. Good, bad, or indifferent I did not then care. The only thing that mattered was that I was rid of it. The relief, the sense of emancipation, was inexpressible. It was finished ; I had done it ; in three months I had written a novel ; and so a sense of achievement intermingling subtly with this glorious feeling of freedom, I began to row, to fish, to climb those mountains to my heart's content.

But now, gradually, through this afterglow of triumph, realization slowly came that the labour of writing the book was not quite everything. There was, for example, the minor matter of publication. I hadn't thought of that before. I felt myself at a very real disadvantage, as I had no friends in the Press, no influence in the world of letters. I knew none of those pashas whose advertisements blazon the pages of literary supplements, and so I was obliged to choose a publisher at random. My conception of a publisher was like the young James Barrie's idea of an editor—a godlike creature approachable only by lesser deities. I was very much afraid that this omniscient being might not condescend to acknowledge my tentative communications. And so, with this doubt in my mind, I wrote to *four* publishers, asking if they were prepared to read my manuscript. I hoped that, with luck, one out of the four might deign, in a moment of absent-minded graciousness, to reply.

They all replied. I tell you this to explode the fallacy that unknown authors cannot get their manuscripts read. And not only will manuscripts be read. If work has merit at all, it will be accepted. Publishers are not too ruthless, but too kind. They accept far too many first novels, in the same spirit, I suppose, in which racegoers back " dark horses."

In my own case the first publisher stated that he would read my novel ; the second that he would be pleased to read my novel ; the third firm informed me that they would be very pleased to read my novel ; but the fourth, ah, the fourth gentleman—he said that he would be *delighted* to read my novel. He, then, in his courtesy, became my victim. I dispatched the manuscript to him by return of post. Then I deliberately put the whole venture out of my head.

I am not ignorant of the polite fiction of the anxious author rising each morning, with straining eyes and palpitating bosom, to meet the postman ; but, although I will concede that author at the cross-roads, I cannot help to perpetuate the picture of the author quivering at the postman's knock. At any rate, I was not like that. I was aware now, only too sadly, too fully aware of the faults in my work. I knew that it was too long, too ponderous, too thoroughly over-written. I knew that it had no merit but a possible sincerity, that it had not the remotest chance of recognition. And so I made the subject taboo amongst my family. I announced that when this thing—we had fallen into the habit of calling it *the thing*—when this thing returned there was to be no word spoken of condolence or regret.

I was stunned when, a month later, I received word that *the thing* had been accepted. Though

I shall never forget the wild exhilaration of that moment, hours passed before I completely realized my phenomenal luck. Then for some time the whole household was topsy-turvy with excitement. When I calmed down, I decided that I must be very level-headed, and wondered staidly whether the book would sell enough copies to justify postponing my return to medical work in order to write a second novel (now that the first step was taken, I did not dare to contemplate the possibility of giving up my practice altogether).

The events which followed made me feel that at any moment I might wake to cold reality from this delightful dream. The novel was chosen by the Book Society, and has since sold one hundred thousand copies in this country and America. It was translated into six languages. It was serialized and dramatized. And, crowning touch of magnificent unreality, a shop in Bond Street now sports the name of *Hatter's Castle*.

I never pass that establishment without experiencing an inward twinge, but whether it be ecstasy or remorse I cannot tell.

E. M. DELAFIELD

OUT of every ten children who are destined later on to take up writing as a profession, ten probably begin to write in childhood. Out of those ten, nine begin by imitation. I have, here and there, met the tenth child—but I was myself well and firmly entrenched amongst the nine. The origin of the impulse to write springs from the earliest experiences of reading, and in my case, as in that, I suppose, of most imaginative children, the books that I read in childhood coloured the whole of my early years.

So large did their influence loom that I cannot write about my writing until I have first told something of my reading.

It will make a melancholy enough saga, in all conscience, for it is one of the regrets of my life that practically no attempt was ever made to direct my reading intelligently, or to extend it beyond the limits of fiction.

That it *could* have been so extended I have no doubt, for reading was my passion. A few years ago a French governess, who came to us when I was eight years old, told me, with a kind of indulgent horror, how greatly she had been struck by my extraordinary habit, as a small child at the nursery tea-table, of pouncing on the current pot of jam or treacle, solely in order that I might read the inscription—which, in those days, ran to a good many words—of the manufacturers !

I vaguely remember doing it, and also learning by heart, from sheer reading and re-reading, the announcement on a still less picturesque domestic article in daily use. Not only was I utterly incapable of resisting print of any kind, but my passion was stimulated by a restriction that, in these days, must appear an almost incredible one.

I was not allowed to read for more than one hour every day.

I have often thought what an unwelcome regulation this must have been to nurses and governesses, who might otherwise have counted on almost unlimited peace and quiet—but they observed it conscientiously.

This preposterous rule was based, first and foremost, on the theory of the period, that whatever a child most enjoyed doing must necessarily be " bad for " him or her, and secondarily — and more rationally — on the grounds that it could scarcely be called either sociable or well-mannered to sit and read all day long, as I should certainly have done if left to myself. There was also a rather vague idea of " saving my eyesight "—though for what particular purpose I have never yet discovered.

One or two of the results of this system may be guessed at. I evaded it in every possible way, but suffered agonies of conscience in doing so, and ended by being quite persuaded that reading was a form of vice. The last quarter or so of the famous " hour " was invariably spoilt by the dread of hearing the clock strike, and the consequent feeling that one must gallop at full speed through the printed page, so as to get in as much of it as possible.

Those printed pages, unfortunately, almost always consisted of children's story books rather below than above the level of an intelligent child's understanding.

There were exceptions : the novels of Sir Walter Scott, *The Mill on the Floss*, and Lamb's *Tales from Shakespeare* are amongst those I remember best. Not many children possess instinctive selective judgment, and most cer-

tainly I had none. In the same catholic spirit
in which I once, as a child, said, quite truthfully,
that my two favourite "tunes" were "In the
Gloaming" and the Boccherini Minuet, so
did I rank, in my own mind, *Rob Roy* with the
serial stories in the current *Little Folks*. To me
a story was a story. The only kind of story that
I did not care for was of the legendary or fan-
tastic type—a distaste that has persisted to this
day. Otherwise, animals, pirates, everyday children, characters in history, fairies, and knights
of chivalry, were all grist to my mill. If I had a
preference, it was for R. M. Ballantyne's adventure stories—but it was not really a very
marked preference. So far as I was concerned,
reading was what mattered : not one kind of
reading more than any other kind, but just
reading. That is why I regret so much that in
those impressionable years no bent was given
to my highly undiscriminating taste, no standard
set before my immature, but receptive, mind.

It was the same thing when I read French
books, which I did—having the good fortune to
belong to a bi-lingual household—at a very
early age. I would gladly have read anything,
from Racine to Alphonse Daudet ; what I was
actually given were the lively, rather vulgar,

rather sentimental, and highly moral tales of
Madame de Ségur, and the pious novels of
Mademoiselle Zénaïde Fleuriot—the French
Roman Catholic equivalent of the English and
Protestant Charlotte M. Yonge. Practically the
only other French book that I remember avidly
reading—and it was worth all the others put
together—was *Le Petit Dictionnaire Larousse*.

There is no need to stress the point any
further. A passion for reading, and an unfortunate absence of critical faculty, were both
equally mine by nature. It would have been
perfectly possible to use the former to my great
and lasting advantage, and to instil in me the
latter by degrees. It so happened, however,
that neither of these services was ever rendered
to me.

I continued to read madly and indiscrimi-
nately, usually by stealth, and to develop a
fearful guilt-complex on the whole subject of
my love of books. It is perhaps not necessary
to add that I was, if possible, more unaware of
the degrees of merit in poetry than of those in
prose.

I read, because they were there, the *Idylls of
the King*, *Enoch Arden*, *Marmion*, the *Poems of
Jane and Ann Taylor*, two ridiculous little books

called *The Young Reciter*, and a large book
called *1,001 Gems of Poetry*. As far as I can
remember, I thought them all equally interesting, and had no idea that any one of them might
be better, or worse, than any other.

I never read one line of Shakespeare until I
was fourteen or fifteen, and at school—and by
that time I was ashamed of enjoying *Henry V.*,
because the other girls thought it affectation.

Oddly enough, although my reading was so
discouraging and unprofitable an affair, my
attempts at writing were all made much of, and
the impulse was acclaimed as a meritorious one.
Why, I find it difficult to imagine, for few
children can ever have shown less promise of
originality.

One effort, and one only, do I remember as
having any merit. This was the beginning of
a French poem, written when I was eight years
old, when I had been set a composition on the
subject of " Fairy Wishes."

> Si une fée m'apparaissait
> Et me disait, " Que veux-tu ? "
> Bien sûr que je répondrai,
> " Tous les livres qui peuvent être lus."

This had the authentic ring of truth : it was

a genuine wish, drawn from the depths of my infant heart, and it was expressed in reasonably simple language. Perhaps this was because it was written in French, in which my vocabulary was less extensive than in English—for when I wrote in English there was a fearful tendency to call every spade an implement of labour.

Like so many beginners, I was sure that it was much easier to write in verse than in prose. How should it not be, when " love " so conveniently rhymed with " dove," and " I " with " die " ? For—need I say it ?—the only themes that I considered worthy of my attention were Love, Death, and Parting for Ever.

In this connection my mother—who did me the really great service of showing me candidly that she did not admire my excursions into high tragedy—gave me a piece of sound advice.

She told me to write—not in verse—about something of which I had had personal experience.

I had not the slightest idea *why* she wanted me to do this, but was quite willing to try.

The outstanding event of my first eight years, it seemed to me, was a fall from a tree, when I had broken my right arm very badly, and had had it set under an anæsthetic.

I proceeded to reconstruct the whole of this incident on paper as accurately as I could—excepting that my prototype in the story was called Violet, and was very beautiful, with dark eyes and long black hair. She had a slightly inferior sister, called Rose, with fair hair and blue eyes. The tree-climbing, the fall, the broken arm, and the subsequent " cradle " in which the arm was set, were all faithfully dealt with. And then—how characteristically !—my dæmon suddenly took possession of me again.

Violet died of her broken arm.

The story ended in a welter of broken hearts, tombstones, and Rose " remembering for ever more."

It never occurred to me to write down the impression that has always remained with me concerning that fall, as the only one of real interest, although it was at least as vivid to me then as it is now, more than thirty years later.

As I fell, I distinctly remembered Alice falling down the rabbit-hole, and seeing a shelf with a jar on it marked " Marmalade." My own fall, which can scarcely have been of more than eight or nine feet, seemed to me to take ages and ages, and I had time to wonder whether I, also, should see a jar marked " Marmalade."

If I had had the sense to include that intensely vivid impression in my ridiculous story it would have brought into it the element of reality in which it was, as far as I can remember, so wholly lacking.

I have told elsewhere of the " books " that I continually began to write and never finished. The chief of these fragments, the one that survived longest, was called *The Hamiltons*. It was about six lovely sisters with an unkind stepmother—and, one by one, they all died, and I revelled in their enormously prolonged death-bed scenes.

These orgies of gloom lasted until I was about twelve or thirteen. The next phase was an improvement, but only a very little one. I became pompous. My sister and I had a manuscript magazine (which we wrote, edited, read, and illustrated for our own and sole benefit), and to it I contributed articles on Ceylon—where I had never in my life set foot—and literary criticisms, full of very long words, and dreary little essays on abstract subjects. The characteristics that strike me now, on looking back at these early efforts, are both negative ones. They were almost entirely devoid of humour, and they were not in the least sincere, but merely more or less conscious imitations of what I supposed to be a " grown-up " style.

My only redeeming feature as an embryo writer, at this stage, was that I knew, quite clearly and consciously, that what I wrote was bad—although I did not know *why* it was bad.

At about sixteen I found quite another outlet, and did nothing but play the piano—for which I had great facility, but no serious talent;—and for the next five or six years I neither wrote nor thought about writing. Certainly I told myself very long stories about imaginary characters of my own creating, but I saw no connection between that and the writing of books.

A personal emotional crisis, and, immediately afterwards, the utter chaos into which the world of my own generation plunged headlong in 1914, caused me to grow up—suddenly and belatedly.

Acting on my own initiative for perhaps the first time in my life, I volunteered for clerical work at the headquarters of a certain V.A.D. organization. I was accepted, I was sent to lodge in a hostel, and I was told that my services would be paid for at the rate of one pound weekly.

It was independence.

No one now under thirty-five can, in all probability, understand what that meant, in those days, to most of the daughters of the upper-middle classes.

It was emancipation of the most delirious kind. It was occupation, it was self-respect—above all, it was freedom.

One of the results of it all, in my own case, was that I suddenly felt again the desire to write, and—something that I had never felt before—the conviction of having something to say.

One of the sagas of my schoolroom days had been about a girl whom I called Zella. She was a girl who posed and pretended, and told lies in order to impress people. (In other words, she was a projection of one aspect of my own schoolgirl personality.) In my original version, Zella committed suicide—always, to the young, the simple and obvious solution of every difficulty.

When I wrote the story that was afterwards called *Zella Sees Herself*, I had acquired the rudiments of a critical faculty, and I knew that the Zella type of person is an undeveloped person. So I wrote of her between the ages of fourteen and eighteen—and I eliminated the suicide.

There were two deliberate portraits in the book : one was the aunt, Mrs. Lloyd-Evans, and the other the old French *baronne*. Two minor characters faintly caricatured people whom I had known. I wrote the whole thing—about 75,000 words—in the odds and ends of time permitted to V.A.D.s. I also wrote, as a matter of course, regardless of interruptions, noises, or any other inconveniences, and I have always been very thankful for the habit of concentration thus acquired, which has never failed me since.

I read the book, as I wrote it, to an audience of three—my sister and two friends. The younger of the friends astounded us all by saying that " we could probably get it published."

I sceptically handed over the manuscript to her, gave her five shillings for stamps, and said that I wished to hear no more of it until it had been rejected by every publisher in London.

Actually, I heard nothing more for six weeks, when Mr. William Heinemann—whom M. L. had intelligently selected as being likely to be interested in a psychological novel—wrote and told me that he would very much like to publish it " after the war."

I have that letter still.

Long afterwards, I learnt that the manuscript, which I had called *Equipment*, was read by Miss F. Tennyson Jesse, and that it was she who recommended it for publication. Mr. Heinemann, quite reasonably, objected to the title as being a misleading one in war-time, and it is also to Miss Tennyson Jesse that I owe the excellent title that the book was eventually given, *Zella Sees Herself*.

I had purposely used a pseudonym, as my own name—de la Pasture—was identified with another writer's very successful and popular plays and novels.

At first I had chosen van der Veldt—the Dutch version of the French de la Pasture and the Flemish van der Weyden. Mr. Heinemann thought it had too Germanic a sound, and my sister suggested Delafield. I kept my own initials—E. M.

But when Mr. Heinemann accepted my novel he did not know anything about me—either my name, or my relationship to " Mrs. Henry de la Pasture."

I went to see him—he was kind but alarming —and implored him not to wait until the war should be over to publish the book. I think

I felt that he might just as well have postponed it till the millennium should arrive.

Eventually the book came out on March 4, 1917, and at the same time, and from the same firm, Miss Clemence Dane's *Regiment of Women* appeared. I have always thought it a brilliant piece of work, and was proud when we were, as often happened, bracketed together by the reviewers.

I had received no advance on *Zella Sees Herself*, and was not by any means certain whether I should ever get any money at all. When I heard that it was going into a second impression, I summoned up all my courage and bleated a timid inquiry.

" Certainly, certainly," said Mr. Heinemann benevolently. " It would be a convenience to you to receive a cheque ? "

I intimated that it would.

The cheque arrived next day, and was for fifty-four pounds odd.

I had expected about fifteen at the very outside.

It is fair to add that for each of the next two novels I wrote I received from Mr. Heinemann a most respectable advance.

Into my second novel, *The Pelicans*, I put

much more autobiography than I had into *Zella*. Half-way through, I had an idea for a purely topical story—*The War-Workers*. It was to depict surroundings and experiences that at that date were more or less familiar to almost every girl and young woman in England.

Mr. Heinemann, when I told him about it, urged me to drop *The Pelicans* and get *The War-Workers* written as quickly as possible, and since any suggestion from one's publishers seemed to me the equivalent of a Royal Decree, I at once obeyed.

The War-Workers, in my opinion, had a much greater success than it deserved. The scenes that depicted the women's hostel, the types met there, and the conditions of living, were accurately and, I think, amusingly sketched, but the love interest, that I put in purely because I thought the story too slight, was bad, imitative, and sentimental.

If I had known my job properly, I should have made of *The War-Workers* a series of sketches, with the slightest possible connecting thread running through them. And I should have omitted the purely conventional and quite insincere attitude that I saw fit to adopt on the subject of women's work.

76

I made, in fact, over *The War-Workers* very much the same mistakes that I made at nine years old, in writing the story of Violet and the broken arm.

One other point. It may seem incredible, but it is an absolute fact, that it never seriously occurred to me that the book would ever be identified with the particular organization for which I was working even while I wrote it.

Of course it was, but I may add that it was also identified, equally positively, with at least a dozen other organizations, of which I had never so much as heard.

Anyhow, I got into a good deal of trouble about it, and perhaps it served me right. But I can honestly state that, whatever I may have become later, I was at that time fool rather than knave !

With the publication of *The Pelicans*, my third novel, properly speaking, these reminiscences should come to an end.

I suppose the actual motives that led me to write are common to most writers who are not, and will never be, in the inspired class. I wanted a form of self-expression, I had inherited a certain facility for writing, and my early obsession for the printed word led me naturally into writing.

Plot and construction have always been my weakest point, but when I began I did not even realize that. Criticism has helped me enormously, and I have almost always found that *reviewers know what they are writing about*, and deserve more gratitude than they often get, especially from beginners.

It will be obvious, if not from the internal evidence of my works themselves, then at least from this article, that I can lay no claim to having formed my style on any of the great models, or been influenced by high and idealistic motives, in writing.

All that I have tried to do is to observe faithfully, and record accurately, the things that have come within my limited range.

The fault that I have most tried to avoid is sentimentality.

LOUIS GOLDING

I DID not lisp in numbers, for I inherited from my father a very clear articulation. He was a *maggid*, a sacerdotal orator, by profession, and I inherited from him also an almost ecstatic love of the Word for its own sake. The Word—the word is used not so much theologically as physiologically—meant almost the same thing to me written or spoken. I still do not see it without simultaneously hearing it. When I heard my father orating in dusking synagogues on Sabbath evenings, in the loveliest, the most bell-like of all remembered voices, the words took shape before my five-year-old eyes. They were jets of water, they were stalks of grass, they were heavy paving-stones.

I composed a poem not long after, for it was inevitable I should soon be playing about with words on my own account. It was a good poem, spontaneous in feeling, revolutionary in technique, and it had actuality. It went :

> He got a big smack,
> And said he'd go back
> To school—
> The fool !

I was proud of that poem. So was my mother. My father was indifferent to it. I am not sure whether I could read or write yet. It was carried about in my head as the minstrel carried his lays.

My first written poem was very literary, and definitely inferior. It ran like this :

> Alone I walked, I walked alone.
> My twitt'ring bird on high I heeded not.
> I heeded not my flower pompous grown,
> And at my twitt'ring little brook
> I gazed not, nor e'en gave a look
> Of fondling . . .

The spelling must have been less exact, but I have lost the original manuscript.

It was largely the intractability of that poem which turned me into a novelist. First of all there was the line, " I gazed not, nor e'en gave a look . . ." It was as odious to look at as to listen to. I tried to adapt it in one way and another, but it remained obdurate. Further, the poem stopped without coming to an end. It could not continue itself. I beat my head against a stone wall suspended in mid-air.

And then my sister, Janey, read me aloud a poem by another writer. It was called " The May Queen." That concluded my rout along two lines of attack. In the first place I realized that no poet ever again could achieve such fluency and flexibility. In the second place, it made me cry my eyes out. I despised myself. I said, if that is the effect of poetry, I've finished with it. I shall be a fireman, or a millionaire, or Dr. Saul in Cheetham Hill Road, but I shall be no poet.

I did not consciously make up my mind to be, on the contrary, a novelist, until I met a certain old lady in a train. We were going to a place called Glossop, I think. My companions had crowded into another compartment, and I was alone with the old lady. I considered her quite a nice old lady, until she addressed me as " little man." " And now, little man," she said, " what are *you* going to be when you grow up ? "

I resisted violently the temptation to stick my tongue out at her. And this I did by concentrating on the subject she had propounded, a subject which had only vaguely occupied me before. What, after all, was I going to be when I grew up ? And then, suddenly, the decision crystallized. I knew in that moment there was nothing else I wanted to be, or was capable of being. " I'm going to be an aufor." " Aufor " definitely meant " novelist." I had had quite enough of being a poet, as I have said, for the time being.

" And what are you going to write ? " asked the old lady.

My reply was instantaneous. " Circus tales. And school tales." And then, as if I was aware that those were not the highest achievements of authorship, I qualified, " But wiv a moral ! "

It may be as a result of my reaction from that early avowal that I have never consciously saddled my more mature works with a moral, and that I have never attempted either a circus tale or a school tale, with or without a moral. My first attempt in fiction followed not long after.

I suppose that its diction and form were dictated by the boys' magazines I read avidly at that time, in which there was always a busy traffic in the market-place during school playtimes—I mean such stalwart weeklies as the *Marvel*, *Pluck*, the *Union Jack*, the *Boys' Friend*, some of which survive to this day, I believe.

My first novel, then, was entitled *The Advenchers of Three on Bludy Island*. The three were the captain, the engineer, and the cabin-boy, on the model of the triune heroes of my magazines. The novel plunged *in medias res* with a promptness and vividness which I have sought in vain to emulate in more mature endeavours in fiction. It opened, like *The Tempest*, in the midst of a howling storm. Thunder crashed. Lightning spat. Waves roared sky-high. And at the very heart of the storm a ship was seen driving inevitably against the rocks. I remember the unction with which I conceived and set down the word " inevitably." I reported it both to my mother, who was as pleased with it as I, and to Miss Brown, my teacher, who had one of her attacks of stomach-ache, and was less impressed.

But there were one or two climaxes to come. In the crash against the inevitable rocks the ship foundered with all hands, except for the captain, the engineer, and the cabin-boy, who, amid the seething ruin, managed hastily to rig up a raft. But, alas, hardly an hour later, the undiminished seas washed the cabin-boy over-board. The storm raged for six days and nights, and then, on the seventh, miraculously subsided. The tropic sun shone in a cloudless sky. Thereupon the captain and the engineer busied themselves with a fishing-rod and a length of twine which they had fortunately salvaged from the wreck along with certain other equipment. The line was cast. " And what were they fishing for ? " I remember the oratorical question vividly, and the triumphant reply : " They were fishing for a human life." In an hour or two there was a jerk on the line. The cabin-boy was hooked. He was lifted to the surface and placed on the raft. Artificial respiration was applied to him, and, three-quarters of an hour later, he opened his eyes again with a gentle sigh. He was in perfect condition, excepting for the fact that a shark had bitten off his left calf.

Subsequent adventures were less exciting, I think. They soared no higher than a forest fire and an earthquake. There was also a subterranean cavern with a river roaring through it. That cavern obsessed a good deal of my early verse and prose. Its origin was our coal-cellar which the river Irwell systematically flooded. Later on, it borrowed dignity and sonority from " Xanadu " :

> Echoes of a distant torrent swelled the harsh, uncertain
> roar
> Of a subterranean river rushing deep for evermore

84

'Neath the ground that shook and quivered while that
    restless river rolled,
Lapping with a restless murmur humid caves of
    sunless mould.

On reflection I am wrong in saying that I did
not attempt a school novel. The successor to
The Advenchers of Three on Bludy Island was a
chapter, but only one, of *The Advenchers of
Another Three*, this time at St. Marylebone's.
The heroes were the son of a fox-hunting squire,
of an Argentine rancher, and of a Jewish
financier. I only remember the name of the
third. It was Rothschild. I was at particular
pains to point out that the fortunes of Rothschild
père were made not by sharp dealing but by
honest labour. There must have been a note
of tendentiousness in that insistence, so that,
within those limits, there was a moral to that
tale. The story collapsed under the pyramid
of Master Rothschild's impossible virtues. I
did not attempt a financier again till I evoked
a certain Smirnof many years later, and he was
only half a Jew.

The first phase of my novelistic career
ended when I was about ten or eleven, with
an Alpine-climbing novel. But I had climbed
so few Alps that my narrative petered out for

want of material. I was not sorry. I had been reading Shelley and Edgar Poe rabidly for some time, particularly Edgar Poe, and under this compulsion I returned to my first love, poetry.

I still engaged publicly in the practice of prose. I had moved to the Southall Street Elementary School, where they taught French, and there was hope therefore that I might win a scholarship to the Manchester Grammar School. A Mr. Ashworth was the teacher of Standard VII., and I owe more than I shall ever be able to estimate to his sympathy and his swift intuition. I wrote essays for him, which gave him more pleasure than they gave the class. He read them aloud, and discovered virtues in them which I had not suspected, and which embittered my classmates. I had not even intended them, for I had grown contemptuous of prose. Night after night, for long hours after midnight, to the crepitation of black beetles between the wall and the wall-paper, I wrote long, labial, melancholy poems. I share a vanity common to most writers. I, too, am convinced that no poems since the invention of writing were as bad as my early love-poems. They were all about maidens

called Laremia, Lenoria, Loramia. Loramia
was a frequent maiden.

> Loramia was a winsome maid,
> Loramia was my bride;
> She left me for a stranger's smile,
> And she crossed the ocean wide
> —Loramia, cruel, cruel!

By this time I had won my scholarship to
the Manchester Grammar School. I remember
a forlorn attempt to publish a volume of poems
in collaboration with the first of my literary
friends, Maurice Samuel, who subsequently
became a novelist and orator of note in the
United States. I remember the exquisitely
tactful way in which J. L. Paton, my High
Master, tackled the situation. He made the
agony of the failure just bearable. I was
driven into a poetry more mournful and horrific
than before:

> Zarda's plains are stained, alas!
> Woe betide—ah! woe betide!
> Green before, now red the grass!
> Ah! woe betide!

It went on like that for a good many stanzas,
with the substitution for " Woe betide,"
of " Lackaday," " Welladay," and " Woe is

me." Woe was me for quite a long time to come, till the High Master induced the editor of *Ulula*, the school magazine, to print a poem by a writer who somewhat crudely disguised his identity under the pen-name "Gholedynge." I ran home from school that day carolling blithely, waving the little blue sheet like a banner. My mother gave me a dish of whin-berries in sour cream. She was proud of her small poet.

I was destined not to read to her many more of my poems. Some months later she became seriously ill, and almost before we realized it was not she who was scouring the brasses or cooking the Sabbath evening dinner, it was clear she would be dead in a week or two. I said to myself fiercely, " I will make her death bearable by writing a great poem about her life and death." And long nights after she died I sat up to make her lovely for ever in octo-syllabic couplets. It was a lengthy poem, but the grief was longer. I managed to make the circumstances of her death less desolate by exteriorizing them and giving them precise shape in my first novel, *Forward from Babylon*.

At this period, or earlier, I made the acquaintance of a poet from Derbyshire — stalwart, genial, melancholy, delicate. His name was

Thomas Moult. He had already achieved some success both as poet and tale-writer. His house in Sedgley Park was an escape from my magnolian slum into fresh air, music, and, above all, the keen winds of critical discussion. He and his wife gathered a group of young writers about them, whose ultimate expression was to be the monthly magazine called *Voices*, the first magazine of the creative arts to appear in England after the Armistice. The surgery performed upon my dreadful poems by that mordant and hypersensitive little company was most valuable.

My slightly chastened poems kept on appearing in the school magazine, but my first bow to the wide world was made, somewhat surprisingly, in the pages of the *British Weekly*. Once again I struck the elegiac note. The poem celebrated the virtues of a great and good man, the father of my High Master. But my first professional piece of work, in the sense that it was actually paid for, appeared in a much more turbulent magazine than the *British Weekly*, published a long way away, at the other end of Europe. This was the *Balkan News*, published in Salonica during its occupation by the Allied troops. The poem enshrined a false quality of which no ex-Salonican ever feels ashamed,

The Shadows Walk Salónica. I received ten drachmas for it. It was distinguished and thrilling that it should be in drachmas I should receive my first literary payment. I bought a chased silver bracelet in the bazaar for a young lady called Kathy. I should like to think she still wears it occasionally.

Was that my beginning? Was the poem in *Ulula*, more than half a decade earlier, my beginning? Or should I say I began with the prose sketches that were accepted for the back page of the *Manchester Guardian*, when I returned from Macedonia? I only know that I should be as proud to have the last words I am destined to write published on the back page of the *Manchester Guardian* as I was to have those early sketches nearly two decades ago. Moreover, even so long ago, I had a sense that those sketches would not stop there. I had not finished with them, nor they with me. They were like isolated strokes in a large crayon cartoon which was to take shape slowly, over many years. They are explicit in the substance of my two large-scale Doomington novels, *Magnolia Street* and *Five Silver Daughters*, which, but for them—but for those brief back-page sketches —would not have come into existence.

WYNDHAM LEWIS

BEGINNING with pen and brush, the penman and the painter are apt to clash; but in my own case this did not occur, when at a very early age these two personalities first came on the scene. Indeed, they made their appearance arm-in-arm, as though they had always cohabited and neither could quite conceive of life without the complementary presence of the other. Indeed, at first, until the fact was pointed out to me, I swear I did not notice that there were *two* familiars there instead of one!

I speak here, of course, as a writer. And I can affirm, I think, that I was so *naturally* a painter that, when I first took up my training, the penman went his own way undisturbed—*bousculant*, certainly, from time to time, and on occasion, the artist in oils and ink (and vice versa, for the penman would sometimes find himself for months together prevented from plying his trade, but that did him no harm—he was all the better for the rest); but on the whole the *homme plume* existed upon perfectly amicable terms with the other occupant of this mortal establishment.

No doubt that was partly a question of equilibrium. When a painter is also a writer, whether good or ill should ensue, artistically, upon this double birth—this twinship in the fashion of Siam of the literary and the plastic executant—depends upon how these partners are mutually balanced. With me, I am inclined to claim, the equilibrium was practically perfect. My best picture, I believe, is as well done as my best book.

Constant association with a person of another but kindred craft could hardly fail to be profitable to both the craftsmen concerned: unless one, it should be found, were overpowered by the other. Given this equality, it must be to the good. Had, for instance, Robert Louis Stevenson lived in intimate association with Paul Gauguin—to select two men of very similar genius, and each pulling about the same weight in their respective worlds—the alliance would have been a great success, I should say; although, in the case of that particular pair, rather harmoniously negative perhaps. Their beach-combing and lotus-eating would have precluded, it is possible, even that minimum of mild friction—of healthy stir and pother—that is requisite to keep the waters of life sweet. With them things would have been *too* absolutely Pacific !

The most notorious instances of duplicated talent, for painting and writing, that is, are, for the Englishman, William Blake and Dante Gabriel Rossetti. Blake's especial hero, Michelangelo, was another. It may be worth while to make a few remarks as to how these tandem-talents functioned, and how, as a rule, one is liable to affect the other.

What we principally notice in each of these artists is that in the two mediums employed by them, literature and painting, their genius is equally powerful. And what can be laid down as an invariable law is that this double life, to be successful, has in truth to be thoroughgoingly *double*—one mode must not merge in, or encroach upon, the other. This it is extremely important to understand.

Blake, as a poet, is far more powerful than Rossetti as a poet ; and the best of his pictures is far more powerful than anything done by Rossetti. But neither of them was really suc-

cessful in his dual rôle, because their two selves
were upon too intimate terms with one another.
In the Rossettian Woman—as celebrated in the
Miss Siddall pencil-drawings—resides, no doubt,
Rossetti's most enduring claim to celebrity.
They are a higher expression of the beautiful
intelligence of this extraordinary man than are
the sonnets he committed to the grave, when
the original of the delicate drawings died, in a
somewhat sinister manner. He should have
sacrificed all the drawings, too, still in his
possession, to have been consistent. He drew
better than he wrote, as it turned out; but
there is, in fact, the same quality and degree
of excellence in the sonnets and the pencil-
drawings. (The paintings are altogether inferior.) In the two arts to which they respec-
tively belong the pictures and the poems are
upon a similar plane of achievement—far beneath the *Songs of Innocence*, or Blake's drawing
of *The Morning Stars Singing Together*.

It is impossible to imagine—and this is what
I am trying to enforce in order to throw some
light, I hope, into what is an obscure corner, for
most critics, of the natural history of genius—
it is quite impossible to imagine Rossetti the
painter (responsible, as he was, for the series of

pencil pieces of the anæmic English Rose—who broke his beautiful Italian heart when she sank into death like a languid and unhappy alien dream) being also responsible, in the art of literature, for the poem commencing :

> " Tiger, tiger, burning bright
> In the forests of the night."

There was nothing of such sinewy substance as that in his nature : you cannot be one man in one art and another in another, though you must certainly be the painter when you are painting, and the word-man (or *homme plume*) when you are writing. And it held good for one art as much as for the other that this romantic and sensuous dreamer had had imposed upon him not only a certain compass, but also a certain type of self-expression. Whether perfectly or imperfectly expressed (and in painting it was very imperfect), his genius directed him to not only a similar eminence, but also to a particular climate and region. And that is the rule.

In a word, there is no such thing as a great poet who, if he gave up some time to producing pictures, would not produce pictures with *some* quality in them that only a great poet could be possessed of—however murkily it might shine forth through an imperfect technical equipment. W. B. Yeats, who began life as a painter, would, had he persevered, have produced *something* with a vague but authentic likeness to his finest poems ; J. W. M. Turner's poems were in reality a criticism of his paintings ; Mr. Joyce's *Chamber Music* or *Pomes Penny Each* should give the critic a foothold from which to survey to advantage the panorama of *Ulysses* ; D. H. Lawrence's pictures (as exhibited in the Warren Gallery) were quite competent enough to betray many secrets of the writer of *The Woman Who Rode Away* or *The Plumed Serpent* ; and the pen-sketches of Charles Baudelaire were of a deliberate, vigorous, and imposing quality, which could leave no doubt in any one's mind that had he devoted more time to pictorial art he would have excelled in it as he did in literature, and upon similar lines—though, naturally, the result might not have been so fortunate. There is the Man, and then there is the Moment. With the *Fleurs du Mal* goes an immortality that paintings corresponding to them, done at that time, might not have brought him. The habits of the literary life may have suited him better, again. There are many things in the world besides this or that talent or predisposition. There is a time to paint a picture, and there is a time to compose an epic in prose.

But I have forgotten Michelangelo. Well, there again you have a poet of the first rank ; not in output to be compared, certainly, with the immensely industrious painter and sculptor —the poetic output is nothing ; but conveying the same reflection of a high imagination. There are people to be found, even—in spite of the marvellous abundance and facility of his creations in the plastic arts, and the reverse in the literary—who prefer Michelangelo the poet. On the other hand, although the poems prove him to have been the intellectual peer of Dante, the poems alone would not have given him in literature the place possessed by Michelangelo Buonarroti in the art of painting.

From all this it will emerge, I hope, that most such questions as : " Which art do you prefer— painting or writing ? " addressed to a writer who is at the same time a painter, or contrariwise ; or all such remarks as " So-and-so is a *better* this than he is a that " (advanced in connection with a dual personality in the arts) is somewhat superficial. The only question that is sensible and not entirely beside the point is : *Which have you done the most of?* or *To which have you devoted most time and energy?* But this is usually obvious, anyway : so those questions, too, are unnecessary.

If you have regarded this preamble as needlessly dilatory, where I am supposed to have set out to inform you " How I began to write," you have, I can assure you, not allowed sufficiently for the especial difficulties in which a writer who never has had a half-finished canvas far away from the desk at which he wrote—who possesses a twin brother in another art—must find himself if interrogated as to " how he began."

For he began, at least that was the case with me, in a painting academy. He wrote his first short story (if the writer in question is the author of *The Apes of God*) while he was painting the subject of it with hog-hair brushes, in petrol quick-drying medium, if I remember rightly ; and the short story was shorter than the painting, I believe I should be correct in saying, in the matter of the time that it took to write. The short story referred to here is one of those to be found in *The Wild Body*.

Technically, then, the short story, as we call

it, was the first literary form with which I became familiar; and I think I may say that the dramatic necessities of this form of art were immediately apparent to me—namely, that *action* is of its essence. And acquainted as I was with both French peasants and English villagers, I chose the former deliberately, because I have always considered that my turn of mind is better suited by the spectacle of people to whom the fundamentals of life are still accessible. Also, I like a wild and simple country, with a somewhat inhospitable skeleton of rock. And if I have not gone to seek these conditions in such parts of these islands as may be found to provide them, it is largely on account of the incessant deluges of water that fall from the Britannic firmament, or because of the detestable Scotch mists that continually conceal everything, and which cause one to become a walking sponge. This is partly owing to an innate dislike for rain, and partly it is, beyond any question, due to the professional reactions of the painter to a climate where he is continually checkmated by poor visibility or by a downright night-by-day. But I very much enjoy the sun as such—apart from any complex reasons for avoiding as far as possible the rain.

When I go to a film like *The Men of Aran*, I shudder at what I see: I recognize that the dry intervals in which it was possible to shoot the film must have been very few and far between; and this pall of rain (into which I have passed many times, on board incoming liners, both from Africa and from America) which stands over England fills me with a hideous melancholy. Rain and no snow! The absence of snow is, if anything, worse than the presence of the rain! Coronation Gulf or the Bay of Whales can be contemplated with pleasure, at least by me. But Aran or the Hebrides! However, I will expatiate upon this no longer. Why my short stories must occur in other parts of Europe, then, or perhaps in the sub-tropical belts, is climatic mainly. I would rather have written *On an African Farm* than *Wuthering Heights*, because in order to write the latter one would have to exist for many years in a perpetual drizzle. To write the former one would at least have to live in uninterrupted sunshine for a considerable length of time.

It was the sun, a Breton instead of a British, that brought forth my first short story—*The Ankou* I believe it was: the Death-god of Plouilliou. I was painting a blind Armorican

beggar. The " short story " was the crystalliza-
tion *of what I had to keep out of my consciousness
while painting*. Otherwise the painting would
have been a bad painting. That is how I
began to write in earnest. A lot of discarded
matter collected there, as I was painting or
drawing, in the back of my mind—in the back
of my consciousness. As I squeezed out *everything* that smacked of literature from my vision
of the beggar, it collected at the back of my
mind. It imposed itself upon me as a complementary creation. That is what I meant by
saying, to start with, that I was so *naturally* a
painter that the two arts, with me, have co-
existed in peculiar harmony. There has been
no mixing of the *genres*. The waste product of
every painting, when it is a painter's painting,
makes the most highly selective and ideal
material for the pure writer.

Tarr was my first published book. It is a
novel. It was first published during the war ;
and I wrote it during the first year of the war,
while I was ill for six months, off and on, and
preparing for the worst. It was a rather ridiculous illness. It hung about for some time,
but was not serious. When the last coccus
took itself off, I knew I should then become a

soldier in the natural course of things (I had no conscience with which to " object "), and already my late companions of peace-time were dying like flies. I naturally assumed that it was quite on the cards that I should take the same road as they and rejoin them in quite a short while now in a better world—it was at least not unlikely. It was very much with this in mind that I took up my pen one day to write my first novel—perhaps my *only* novel, I said to myself. I wished to leave behind me a little specimen of my hand, that was the idea—upon the big scale, in a great literary form, to show the world—should I in my turn succumb—what a writer it had lost ! A romantic consideration ! But the war, as it descended upon us, made romantics of us all, I think, if we were not romantics already. I had, however, in the back of my head a great accumulation of that matchless literary material, that waste product I have mentioned (flung back in his toil by the uncompromising painter). It did not take long to spin my plot. And there I lay, writing of Huns and Hunesses, without at all understanding the political symbolism of my action, while the Hun was hammering at the door, encamped almost at Calais.

I thought of no great paragon of style when first I dipped my pen in the ink and put *Knackfuss* for *Montparnasse* (thus germanizing Paris): I was in far too great a hurry to do that. There was no time to consult the great masters of manners. Such manner as I possessed was my own. I entered writing with a careless tread. Nay, I bolted into literary composition—there was some arrogance perhaps in my invasion of the literary field. There were the circumstances; but if the tailor had not been impatiently in attendance to measure me for my British Warm, so to speak—if I had had a world of time in which to turn round and pick a pilot—it would have been just the same.

V. S. PRITCHETT

FEELING my way back into the past, like one groping through a wood in the darkness, I cannot find the place where the belief of vocation as a writer first came to me. I can trace it to my tenth year and, less surely, to my fifth. Probably it is to be found in the first three years, which the Jesuits and the psychologists say are the decisive ones. There, at this time, came those first tremors of that sense of isolation—they call it maladjustment—which, ever heightening, becomes the abiding characteristic of the writer's temperament. But this morbid theory of art is too deep for me. If it is true, then my grandfather and father were artists without knowing it. And not only they but my maternal grandmother's " brother Gil," of whom I was said to be " the spitting image," and who was a cheerful fishmonger, always stopping his cart in the road to tell his latest story.

Both my grandfather and my father were men

of egotistical and romantic nature, who loved words. My grandfather's isolation was the more dramatic, for he was one of the few men who declare they have heard the voice of God. He was a soldier, and he was court martialled and dismissed from the army for sending a cannon ball through the sail of a yacht at gunnery practice. Overcome, and yet defiant in his disgrace, he became a labourer on the roads, and it was there that the voice of God told him clearly that there was an Authority beyond the authority which had punished him, and that he was chosen to be the mouthpiece of this ultimate greatness. He threw down his pick, and although he had a wife and two children and no money, he turned himself into a student, taught himself Greek in his tram journeys to and from the theological college, and in due time became a Congregational minister. He was a short, stout, violent man, with a harsh voice, militant, kindly eyes, and a beard. Hell sounded imminent when he spoke, and Heaven stupefying. He composed his sermons on the earth closet at the end of his garden, while cigar smoke poured over the top of the door. He was a man defiant yet meditative, and apart.

Like many egotists who, on the whole, dislike their adult fellow creatures, my grandfather liked children. At least he loved me, and I, though I was afraid of him, loved him. I often genuinely feared, for example, that he might eat me. But there were books in his house, and he had some interest in ideas. I have wondered if I became a writer, because he would say, as he stamped down the Yorkshire roads working off the violence of a nature which the voice of God had tricked into becoming sedentary : " Now, John Ruskin—there's a fine man for you." Or, " Marcus Aurelius—what a man ! " When I was born he earnestly hoped my mother would call me Marcus Aurelius ; but my mother had the fishmongering tradition and was wise.

As for my father, he had a small stationer's shop and a post office when I was born—both plausible omens. On the other hand, he soon left them for other shops and businesses up and down the country. A persuasive tongue and infectious optimism made him into a celebrated commercial traveller in that most dismal of trades—the drapery ; until he too achieved the apartness he desired—the creation of his own business. I read the other day that Mr. H. M.

Tomlinson, when once told he should visit a certain Buddhist temple because it was unique, replied : " No.   So am I unique."   My father would admire Mr. Tomlinson for that retort ; and, such is the durability of the Nonconformist tradition, I think I too admire Mr. Tomlinson's sinful pride.

It will be no surprise to the psychologist to be told that I, who am lean, have always been greatly influenced by stout men, and that after my grandfather and father, the next stout and decisive influence was a schoolmaster, a man of genius, who taught me for three years at his school.

My father's commercial struggles left us poor. There were few books in the house.   There was a cheap Shakespeare, a couple of novels by Marie Corelli and one by Hall Caine, a book of sermons called *Brooks by the Traveller's Way*, a scarlet book on paper-bag cookery, and a green volume called *Marriage on Two Hundred a Year*, which made my mother angry when it was quoted to her.   We lived in London and I was sent to a board school.   Here a class of sixty boys and girls, many from the near-by tenements, were given the foundations of a literary education whose richness, liveliness,

and evocative power was never touched at the
humdrum public school to which I was later on
sent until I was sixteen years old.   But at this
earlier school, though it made the question of
writing one of intense and public conviction for
me, my instinct for isolation received its first
shock.   The master made us all write—all
those others who had no right to the voice!
They wrote essays, stories, and criticism, easily
outdoing mine.   They invented.   They imagined; or, at least, they imitated with resource
and skill.   And, years later, it was the same.
I was not alone in having written a novel of
genius at the age of eleven!   Even the girls
had done this.

Ardently determined upon being the unique
one—I know I am betraying myself to my
reviewers who always manage to get a good
meal out of my idiosyncrasies—I decided to
leave prose and plump for poetry.   " Diana,
Goddess of the Spectre Moon " was the result.
It was followed by a " Lament of the Wives,"
a stretch of blank verse declaimed by the women
of a Spanish town, when they go out at night
to search the battlefield for the bodies of their
husbands—for the Spanish setting see *Children's Encyclopædia* :   article on the Alhambra.

" The Lament " was seen by nobody because of the disastrous effect of " Diana " on the class. I rushed to school with it. I wanted to declaim it to all. When the master took it I sat trembling in my desk, pretending to work, but watching his face as he read. He said nothing. It had rained in the morning, and I remember the asphalt of the playground was like a mirror when I went out at playtime and lingered near the master, hoping for the word " genius " to come from him. He seemed to avoid me. I came nearer, so near that at last he had to speak. He was a stout man, with a thick neck and big, chalky hands. In the least dramatic, gravest, most sardonic, and casual way he said, " Your poem is obscure, because it is too ambitious and you use long words."

As my grandfather stupefied his congregation with his description of heaven, so did I stupefy the class with my " Diana." Boys were uncomfortable when they mentioned it. But it made for me an excellent enemy. He was a skinny, underfed, shabby, red-haired boy called " Ginger." He sold newspapers after school. He was a gifted squib of a child, a fast runner who got under every one's feet. He jumped up and down like a cracker, sparkling with gibes.

He was a fiend. He flattered me until I showed him my latest works, and then tore them to bits, punctured my windiest metaphors, argued my emotions out of existence, mocked my bad rhymes and scansion ; and when I tried to end his subtle intellectual persecution by clouting him, he skipped out of the way like a stinging fly. He vied with me in everything. Our life was a series of leaps to outstrip each other. " Ginger's " family were very poor, and I think hunger sharpened his natural intelligence. I admired him and despised him for his poverty, and I think if I had been as poor as he, he would not have been so impelled to take it out of me. The thing which really bound us together was that we were the smallest boys in the class.

Once the decision to be not a mere writer but a poet was made, I added a new sentence to my prayers. First I said, " Gentle Jesus, meek and mild " slowly, with a feeling of holy exultation. Then, more urgently, I usually asked that the house should not catch fire during the night—as that house had done at Torquay —then that it should not be burgled ; then that I should not be kidnapped—a man had tried to kidnap my sister. Now I added the request that I should be Poet Laureate when I was nineteen—no, on second thoughts twenty-one. "Diana," I now believe, had been cribbed from "Christabel"—I had all the *Penny Poets*—and now I had the sensation of being one of the Lake Poets. . . . No one can have suffered as I have from the impossibility of being a Lake Poet. I used even to walk through the miles of suburban streets to the boating lake in Dulwich Park, in order to evoke the dream. I was now so dedicated to poetry that I foolishly boasted of the fact to my brother and sister. The effect was immediate. They stood back and shouted, "Dirty poet." I said poets were dirty because they thought of higher things, but that actually I was a clean poet. My father, who has been always fanatical about cleanliness, looked up at this. He said a dirty man always got the sack. He also said, a remark which depressed me for years, that you should tell a man's character by his boots. His father, he said, had always told him that. One morning my father came into my room and caught me reading *Measure for Measure*. (One was always "caught reading" in our house.) He said he hoped I was not getting the idea into my head that I was going to be a poet. I can understand the hope.

Financial anxiety, constant crises in which—though his appetite was always enormous—he would go without meals to save money, led him to think of the day when we should get out and earn our livings.

Meanwhile, poetry having eased my vanity, I sidled into prose. I wrote an attack on Marie Corelli, because she had written scornfully about popular education and the board schools. My father told me that Marie Corelli was a great writer, and that one of her books had changed his life. So I read *The Master Christian* and for many months one winter I wished to be a blind organist in a church that caught fire, and to rescue a beautiful woman from the flames. I set to work upon a novel.

An awful and humiliating thing now happened which brought me into conflict with my father, and drove all literary dreams into secrecy. Such conflict is inevitable. We were sitting round the table at tea one Sunday. Beside him my father had a paper. I saw at once it was a copy of a boys' paper, chiefly of school stories, called the *Magnet*. I loved the *Magnet*. There were a dozen copies of it in my bedroom. It was clear at a glance that my father hated the *Magnet*. What he really disliked, I think, was the fact that it was a dirty and greasy paper. I bowed my head, waiting for the first cold questions and then the hot denunciation. He started off by telling me to sit up straight. He said I was round-shouldered. Then he said I affected this just to show how learned and superior I was. That was why I was dirty. " A dirty poet," he said. The others laughed. But I wasn't superior, learned, and poetical, he said. I was a fraud. I read all the trash and muck I could lay hands on. " This ! " He waved the gaudy paper in the air.

I was truly horrified. I knew at once that none of the Lake Poets would have read the *Magnet*. They sat—I had no head for dates— beside brooks and wooded fells, deep in their Tennysons and Brownings. I was appalled by the depths to which I had fallen. Obviously I had no vocation. Tears ran down my cheeks. My father softened as his anger declined to a warmer and more discursive plane. He appealed to my higher self. And then he said— going off into a dream—and could not know the effect of his words :

" Now, what about John Ruskin—there's a fine man for you."

I awakened from my shame at the sound of this name. I warmed to my father. My higher nature shone. But the higher nature has an extraordinary way of awakening wiliness too, and, before I knew where I was, I began to boast shyly to get myself back into favour. I boasted that John Ruskin had not been forgotten, for I, too, had written a book. It was a novel.

"You have what?" said my father in a quiet, amused, suspicious, and ominous voice.

I saw my mistake. I tried to pretend I was exaggerating.

"Bring it to me," he said.

I refused. He insisted. I broke into tears again. He told me to stop snivelling. My sister, in a holy voice, said she knew where the manuscript was, and she would get it. Betrayed, I shouted across the table that I would give her one in the chops if she did. Chops, said my father, how dared I use such a word in his house. My mother said I picked it up at that dreadful school. My father said obviously the school was too good for me.

"And bring the rest of these filthy magazines with you," my father said.

I was now crying with misery and shame. I

hated my father. I thought what a hypocrite my mother was to say she loved me and to allow this to go on. I vowed I'd revenge myself on my brother and sister. But they were shaken at seeing their elder brother cry. They thought it might be their turn next.

The moment he took the manuscript my father expanded and smiled. A look of merriment and satisfaction shone on his face. He gloated. And yet he looked very dignified and lofty. The name John Ruskin on his lips had given him an air of spiritual power. Whatever he said, I knew, would be right. Then, to my shame, he began to read aloud.

"Listen to this," he said, with an odd mixture of pride in me and of mockery.

The first chapter of my novel described a scene in one of the courtyards of the Alhambra. A fountain was playing, and to the sounds of music a beautiful woman rose out of the water.

My father raised his fine eyebrows.

"It's all silly. I just did it for fun. It's all stupid," I protested, willing to admit anything to stop him. I knew every word that was coming. I was ashamed (and proud) of every one.

"'Then,'" my father read, "'she adjusted

115

her robe with osten—os—' what's this, my
boy ?—' ostentatious, care.' "

He put down the manuscript.

" Where did you get that word from ? " he
said.

" What's it mean ? " he said.

" Ostentatious," he said. " I have never
seen that one before. What does it mean ? "

No one answered. He pressed me. I lied
and said I didn't know what the word meant.
The dictionary was brought. He read out
" ostentatious : showy."

" Oh," says my father, impressed, " you
spelled it right anyway."

I have forgotten how the episode ended,
except that the *Magnet*, twenty copies of it and
none of them mine, was burned on the fire. It
made a fine blaze. My father liked making
the chimney blaze. My mother sent me out
into the street to see if the chimney was on fire.

In the hours that followed, my face stinging
with the dried tears, I had the feeling of having
been purged by suffering. I felt no longer
holy and separate, but wounded and wise.
Every one became suddenly sympathetic. My
father who had gloated now talked earnestly of
giving me a good education. It was less with a

116

desire privately to revenge myself upon my father, than with a feeling of being older and wiser, that I threw the manuscript into the dustbin next day. But perhaps there was more of revenge in it, the desire " just to show them " in it, than I thought, for my mother said it was a silly thing to do.

After this I gave up all idea of being a writer, at least I held the dream privately, above all kept it from my father. Anyway I could think of nothing to write about, and I pretended I wanted to be a schoolmaster. At my new school foreign languages engrossed me; and once when the desire to write returned and I tried my hand, the master, a bitter and pedantic Irishman, wrote across my book, " From Ruskin, and badly assimilated." He said Ruskin was the worst writer in the English language. He also said I was the worst writer in the form. When he heard that I was to leave school—I was fifteen—and was going to work in a leather factor's warehouse, he said it was just what he had expected. But I stayed another year, and the next master was kinder. He went through his job in a dispirited, mechanical way and left us alone. And under his neglectful tuition I made a discovery—the discovery of the differ-

ence between the romantic dream of writing
and the use of the imagination. To those who
have never been enmeshed in that dreaming
this may seem no discovery. We were told to
describe an air-raid. I was uninterested—no
Lake Poet had ever written on the subject.
And then I remembered my mother's dread of
air-raids; how she called us all down and sat
moaning with her arms round us and her eyes
closed, while we turned our heads, straining to
go to the windows and watch. Suddenly it
occurred to me—why not write as if I were
a woman and very afraid? To imagine and
not to dream! I wrote with great happi-
ness. The master read the thing out to the
class, and said it was the only essay worth
anything.

Naturally I thought now was the time to
come into the open. I had arrived. I told my
father I was going to be a journalist. He was
very put out by this, and he took me to see a
customer of his.

"And what does the young man want to
do?" asked this man.

"He thinks," said my father, "he *thinks* he
wants to be a journalist."

The man laughed.

" Tell him to read *Sinister Street*," he said. " That will cure him."

I was never able to get a copy of this precious book. And shortly afterwards I was sent to Bermondsey to sort skins. There's nothing like leather, people said, when I told them. They always laughed.

The dream returned. I read and worked at night. That is, I tried to work. I sent manuscripts to papers. They all came back, month after month, year after year. It was merciful that they did. No one I knew was interested in literature. I could get no advice. That air-raid revelation did not come again. I sat, smelling of leather, at the dining-room table with the family, reading after supper was cleared away. Now it was Balzac, now Chateaubriand, now *Le Nez d'un Notaire*, and *Gyp*. There were Omar Khayyám, James Barrie, *Comin' Thro' the Rye*, the novels of G. M. Macdonald, and Bacon's *Advancement of Learning*—a muddle of books, a muddle in my mind. How did *they* do it ? How was Milton written ? How *Three Men in a Boat* ? People were reading Lawrence and Proust, and I had never heard of them.

I left leather and went to France on the pretext of getting business experience. Once in that land the thing became easier. People did not grin uncomfortably when I began my tale of how much I wanted to write, but I did not know how. Encouraged, I took to saying I was a writer. I was actually employed in the glue trade, but I let it be understood this was a spare-time occupation. I began to get a reputation as a writer because I said I was one. I spent many hours every night in the Rotonde and the Dome looking like a writer. One evening an American schoolmistress, to whom I was talking, stopped me in the middle of a sentence and said, admiringly :

" What you said just now was an epigram."

I walked home now convinced I was a writer. My friends agreed that I was. And so it came about that seeing in the *New York Herald,* one day, a notice that the paper would publish any good jokes of not more than a hundred words, I thought one out in the next few weeks, and rewrote it several times and sent it to the editor. It was published. And underneath was my full name and address. I was twenty-two. Most people have written their novels by then. And as for poets—it is their old age.

V. SACKVILLE-WEST

THIS essay owes its existence to two facts. First, to the suggestion of my friend, L. A. G. Strong ; and second, to my own hoarding instinct. By my own hoarding instinct I mean my reluctance to throw certain things away. In most people this instinct proceeds from the vague idea that the object in question " may come in useful some day " (which it never does) ; in my case it proceeds from a disinclination to destroy the written page. Thus it comes about that I have quite unnecessarily and rather sentimentally preserved an alarming number of foolscap ledgers representing the literary activities of my early years.

They stand in a row at the bottom of my bookshelves, getting dusty and more dusty as time goes on. I never look into them. A mere glance at their backs is enough to make me blush with shame. Whenever I catch sight of them, I know that I ought to take them out into the garden and make a bonfire. But, as

Mr. Max Beerbohm has pointed out, it is
extremely difficult to burn a book. And here
are many books. They are all in fat ledgers,
stiffly bound in cardboard—the sort of ledgers
which one sees piled in such alluring stacks in
stationers' shops—solid ledgers such as would
defeat even the holocaust of a modern Savona-
rola. I could not face the practical difficulty
of setting them on fire. Besides, there is that
hoarding instinct which makes me shrink from
the final destruction of all that early energy.
So they remain in their harmless, unexamined
row at the bottom of my shelves. I was
content to preserve them and never to look into
them, until Mr. Strong's letter arrived, forcing
me to the embarrassing task of exploring my
literary past.

Then I blushed indeed. I blushed, but at
the same time I couldn't help being slightly
impressed by my own industry and neatness.
I had quite forgotten the neat, industrious, and
priggish child I once had been. All those
conscientious historical notes ; all those in-
sertions in red ink, done with a mapping
pen. . . . Looking into my first big ledger, I
realized that I had worked out my first plays
and my first poems much as I drew maps of

the river system of France for the classes I
attended in London. The mapping pen and
the red ink had come into use for both my
official lessons and my private poetry. The
only difference was that my lessons were merely
lessons, and that my plays, my poetry, and my
novels really mattered to me ; they constituted
the whole of my secret life. Still, the neatness,
the priggishness, and the red ink which per-
meated my lessons were present also in the
writings of my private life.

I must have been an insufferable child : an
impression which has subsequently been richly
confirmed by my then contemporaries.

My parents treated me with creditable intelligence. In fact, my only grievance against
them is that they taught me neither Latin nor
Greek, and never thought of sending me either
to school or to a university. Apart from this
sad omission, they behaved with exemplary
good sense towards the odd duckling they had
hatched out. They neither injudiciously encouraged nor unkindly snubbed. Thus, I
remember that my earliest ambition was to
appear at a dinner-party of thirty people in
the banqueting hall at home, dressed in a sheet
representing a ghost, in order to recite an epic

poem composed by myself on the various
exploits of my ancestors. This proposal, which
must have proved very embarrassing to my
parents, was wisely but amiably suppressed.
A ghost aged twelve, complete with epic poem,
was scarcely a guest to be welcomed at a
dinner-party of thirty grown-ups.

My second venture met with a more sympathetic response. By that time I was fourteen (for these statistics I am indebted to one
of the ledgers I found myself so reluctant to
destroy). Having, at that age, fallen strongly
under the influence of *Cyrano de Bergerac*, and
also of *The Three Musketeers*, I had composed a
tragedy which aspired to combine both the
poetical romanticism of Rostand and the historical romanticism of Dumas. The result—
strange bastard as it was—took the form of a
five-act play on the " Man in the Iron Mask,"
in French Alexandrines. Of French Alexandrines I had but little experience, and still less
technical knowledge. I knew only that an
Alexandrine consisted of twelve syllables to the
line, but knew nothing of the necessary cæsura,
and even less of the mute e. The twelve
syllables, however, which I did know about, became an obsession. Every sentence which I

uttered in ordinary speech, whether in English
or in French, must be shaped into twelve
syllables or their multiple. At first I counted
on my fingers under the table, or behind my
back ; or, when I couldn't conceal my fingers,
I wriggled my toes inside their shoes. It was
very difficult to wriggle one's toes separately,
so I thought of them, one after the other,
instead. But soon my ear grew so well accustomed to the scansion that there was no longer
any need for my fingers or toes to come into
play. This trick was, I suppose, analogous to
the superstitious trick some children have of
stepping on the cracks in pavement stones.
" If you miss a crack you will meet a bear," or
" your sums will not come right." Eleven
syllables, or twenty-three, or forty-seven, were
to me a portent of disaster. I still catch myself
playing this game sometimes.

My five-act tragedy, I fear, was a ludicrous
though ambitious attempt. My parents nevertheless, not having been allowed to read it,
consented to let me act part of it, supported by
a friend to whom was allotted the secondary rôle.
I myself played the part of the Man in the Iron
Mask, dressed in cheap black sateen and a
Vandyke collar of imitation lace. The audience

consisted of my parents and the French servants.
My parents listened patiently; the French
cook, to my extreme gratification, burst into
tears. I felt that I had at last scored a triumph.

My third venture was equally ambitious, but,
luckily for my family, was conducted in greater
privacy. This was a play in blank verse on
the life and death of Thomas Chatterton. I
had the play printed by the local stationer at
my own expense; it cost me £5 for a hundred
copies—£5 which I saved out of my tips and
pocket-money for the year.

The sentiments expressed in this play were
excessively noble. So noble were they, that
I felt impelled to keep them to myself, and
therefore made no attempt to inflict them upon
my family as an audience, but performed them
secretly, and for my single benefit, in an attic
at the top of the house. The attic was a
strangely suitable setting: I realize now that
with its bare boards and latticed window it
must closely have resembled the attic in which
poor Chatterton spent his last tragic days. Of
course I did not realize this at the time. I
realized only that as there was no cook to weep,
I must weep myself, and consequently was
moved to tears every time by my own per-

formance. Each time I burnt Chatterton's manuscripts in the candle I felt I was burning my own; each time I died most uncomfortably on the oak settle, it was not only Chatterton but I myself who died. It was a case of "mighty poets in their misery dead." I especially fancied myself in the costume I had devised for this rôle: black breeches, white stockings, buckled shoes, and a white shirt. Luckily, nobody ever caught me at the game, otherwise I should certainly have been sent straight to bed for having run the risk of setting the whole house on fire.

What next? I remember a whole succession of historical novels, running into at least three hundred pages of foolscap each, all very neat, with dates in the margin, and sometimes the marginal comment V.E.—my private sign, meaning Very Easy; in other words, "It has gone well to-day." These historical novels covered quite a wide range. There was one about Alcibiades; one about the French Revolution; one about Louis XIII. (this one, very Dumas-esque, was written in French, for between the ages of two and eighteen I was what, thank God, I no longer am, bilingual); one about Florence in the fifteenth century, inspired by George Eliot's *Romola*; and at least three others about my own home and my own ancestors. All these I wrote at great speed and with extreme gusto. I kept them very private; and no sooner had I finished one than I started another; sometimes, as their dates inform me, on the very same day.

A little later came a history of the Italian city-states from 1300 to 1500, full of murderous and probably inaccurate detail. I enjoyed this enormously, partly owing to the amount of research it involved, for I had not yet shed the priggishness and pedantry of my school-days. Visconti and Sforza, Scaligeri and Baglione, Sismondi and John Addington Symonds, became my constant companions for two happy years.

Then, tiring of history, whether romantic or factual, I tried my hand at writing a modern novel. I was then twenty-five, and old enough to know better, but prose was still only a contemptible stopgap for the days on which I couldn't write poetry, and of the construction of a novel I knew no more than I had known of the construction of a French Alexandrine. I had, for instance, no idea of the number of words necessary in fiction from a publisher's point of view ; ten thousand words meant no more to me than a hundred thousand. Thus it came about that my first novel, when finished, was only about forty thousand words long. Still, unconscious of the deficiency, it seemed to me very much like a novel ; very much like the novels which other people wrote and which actually got printed. I was rather pleased with it ; so well pleased, that in the first flush of excitement I submitted it to the only publisher I knew—the only " literary " person, in fact, with whom I then had any acquaintance at all. To my delight he consented to read it, only to return it after a week's interval with a kindly worded letter to say that although it showed " considerable promise," it was much too short for publication. So I put it away, disheartened, for a year.

During that year I went to live in Ebury Street. I lived at No. 182, but at No. 121 lived a more distinguished and more experienced neighbour, who had been practising the art of fiction, both in conversation and on paper, for many years, and who fell into the habit of arriving at my house unannounced, after dinner, whenever he had nothing better to do. Conversations in Ebury Street ensued.

They were not so much conversations as monologues ; George Moore enjoyed talking about himself ; but, luckily for me, his monologues in my house usually took the form of literary rather than amorous experiences. He would relate at great length the story of the book he next intended to write : thus I remember listening patiently to the whole proposed scheme of *Héloïse and Abélard*, and *A Story-Teller's Holiday* ; or he would rush into the sitting-room in a state of great excitement, saying " Give me your copy of *The Brook Kerith* at once ; I sought for a phrase of Christ for years, and now at last I have found it—let me write it into your copy, before I forget it." (Incidentally, although he called it a *trouvaille*, it wasn't a particularly illuminating *trouvaille* at all. It was a rather trite, commonplace little phrase.)

Humbly, I was content to listen to George Moore's monologues by the hour, since anybody who had not only written but had actually published many books, was then almost a god to me, or, at any rate, a superior and successful being. Then there came one magical moment when he switched off from himself and condescended to remember my own existence.

" Have you," he said, " ever attempted to write yourself ? A great mistake if you have ; but I expect you have been guilty of that usual indiscretion of the young." He fixed me with a threatening and critical eye. " Come, now," he said, " confess."

I confessed.

Under persuasion, I told him the whole story of my unfortunate novel.

He was charming about it. Not only did he listen with flattering attention, but he even suggested a means by which I might extend it to the necessary length. The means he suggested were due to what he described as " a real-life story " he had read in some American newspaper. Practically every reviewer who subsequently condescended to notice my book observed that nothing of the sort could ever have happened in real life. Thus I am wholly indebted to George Moore for the eventual publication of my first novel.

BEATRICE KEAN SEYMOUR

ONE of my earliest recollections is of myself as a child sitting by the fireside listening to my mother's stories as she busied herself with household tasks. Even more than most children, I would do anything for a story, whether improvized, read aloud, or found within the covers of a book. And although my mother has never written a line of a story in her life, she had, as a young woman, a marvellously exciting and interesting way of telling a story, and her store of narrative always seemed unending.

In a way, I suppose, my genesis as a writer must be reckoned from those now, alas, far-off days when, as a very small schoolgirl, I spent a great deal of time that ought to have been devoted to higher things in concocting tales for my classmates. These were of a highly romantic character, dealing with the hard lives lived by beautiful and saintly little girls who were misunderstood by stern parents, or about naughty, troublesome ugly ducklings who turned out to be clever and achieved fame when they grew up, or sirens who captured millionaires in their extreme youth and lived adored and happy ever after.

These efforts were carefully bound together in booklet form with coloured cotton, and illustrated by my own especial girl friend, who had a definite talent for sketching, and would draw, in pencil or in ink, delectable little girls with lovely heads of hair and the most beautiful legs in the world. Her illustrations, I am quite sure, were infinitely superior to the material they were designed to accompany, and on those rare occasions when we were not on speaking terms, the popularity of my manuscripts suffered severe eclipse. What happened, I wonder, to all that budding pictorial talent ? I never knew, for Fate intervened early to push us along different paths in life.

I do not remember, however, that my share in these proceedings of our extreme youth was either encouraged or applauded by my immediate elders. On the contrary, I seem to recollect that not infrequently it was referred to variously as " Such nonsense ! " and " Waste of time." But my form mistress must have been more sympathetic, I fancy, for I have never forgotten that when one day she asked me what I wanted to be when I was grown-up, and I said, without a moment's hesitation, " An authoress," she was nice enough not to laugh. Perhaps she felt kindly disposed towards a child who, at ten, would relieve the monotony of tutorial existence by beginning an essay upon " Life in the Country and the Town " with this startling phrase : *In these days of cheap and rapid transit* . . .

My first attempt at fiction proper, however, belongs to a rather later day, when I must have been about fourteen, and was asked by the irascible Scotsman with feet like a dancing master, who taught us English, to address myself to the writing of an essay upon the theme of "An Old Shoe." It was part of my inalienable attitude to this business of being a child that I must always do rather more than was required of me (when I did not do a great deal less !), so my essay was about not one shoe but two. And here, I think, a hint of the embryo novelist must have declared itself, for one of them was a female shoe, and the other a male. And both were old and down-at-heel, and they met in the gutter—a pair of inveterate snobs, who lay and recalled their lost grandeurs when, polished and fashionable, they adorned the feet of two of the world's comfortable people.

Born in an age when women's independence was already being taken for granted, I was at no time dismayed by the fact that I had my own way to make in the world ; but as I grew older I was certainly dismayed by the means which presented themselves to me of achieving this laudable end. My mother, for all her story-telling, had a practical mind ; neither she nor my father belonged to families that had fostered leanings towards the arts, and they are not to be blamed for refusing to take my literary ambitions very seriously. To them it was more than anything else essential that I should be trained definitely for some profession within their means, which would ensure me a competence—and a pension for my declining years ! The two favourite openings, I soon discovered, which were believed to lead to these desiderata were teaching and the Civil Service—to avoid both of which, at sixteen, I made a bolt for the schoolroom door. Faced with this *fait accompli*, my parents decided that I had better be sent to a commercial school for a year, where a sound training in the secretarial arts could be achieved. Being a secretary, they assured me, would not interfere with my dreams of authorship.

About this I proved unexpectedly tractable ; but that, I now suspect, was because already I saw visions of my ultimate emergence as the Perfect Secretary, who obtained, miraculously and at once, a congenial, highly-paid engagement with one of the Most Important Writers of the Day, who immediately recognized my quite unusual ability and made it his (or her) business to set my feet firmly upon the first rungs of the ladder to literary fame.

Well, it didn't happen that way. . . .

My next few years were divided between this business of learning to earn a modest living, beginning, in fact, to earn it, studying English Literature at King's College in the Strand, and in going on, in secret and alone, with this (to me) far more important business of learning to write. Like Mr. H. G. Wells, much earlier, I had to get the hang of it—I could never for long leave it alone. I wrote short story after short story, worked over them again and again, typed them neatly, and put them away in a drawer. It never occurred to me to offer them to magazine editors, for I was still in my teens, and in those

days, though it might well be " very heaven,"
in Wordsworth's dawn or any other, to be
young, Youth was not yet the Open Sesame
to the printed page that it has since become.

I sometimes think that those neatly typed
and frequently worked-over manuscripts would
have been the beginning and end of my maturer
efforts at authorship, but for the interest of one
of the masters at my commercial school. A
free-lance journalist in his spare time, he had
been interested in me from the first—partly, at
least, because I recognized the letter " r " when
I saw it in a word, but also because I could
read the shorthand I wrote (a rare accomplish-
ment that, he said), and never wrote nonsense
when I couldn't—an even rarer accomplish-
ment ! Soon after I had joined his class he
had won my shy confidences, and, with difficulty,
had persuaded me to show him some of my
literary efforts. What he found to say of them
I still remember with gratitude as sharp as
upon the day it was called forth. Later, when
my student days were done, a literary weekly
announced a competition for a short story by
a beginner, and my former teacher bullied me
into sending in a tale, written at the mature
age of seventeen, of which he had thought

particularly well. Nobody more surprised than
I, and nobody more proud than he, when it was
awarded the prize !

This effort, luckily, has not been preserved,
but Sir Max Pemberton (then plain Max),
who adjudicated, said some kind and flattering things about it that warmed my young
heart. Success, however, was by no means as
yet sitting upon my doorstep, and my level-
headed parents had every opportunity—and
excuse—for reminding me during the next year
or two that one swallow doesn't make a summer,
or even a summer's day. Gradually, none the
less, I began to add to my income by writing
simple stories of the kind the women's papers
would print for a fee of two or three guineas,
and presently there arrived an exciting day
when I had a story accepted by the *Bystander*
and another by the *Queen*. Later, a new,
serious-minded magazine called the *Magpie*
appeared upon the scene, and, greatly daring, I
sent them a story about the childhood and
adolescence of a girl who was " odd woman
out " in her dull, unimaginative family. To
my great delight this story was accepted, and
in a personal letter the editor expressed his
admiration for it, but " feared it would be

difficult to fit in." A little later I sent him another story, based upon a ghostly experience which had befallen my mother as a young girl, which was printed at once. But the more ambitious effort, upon which all my hopes as a short-story writer were centred, was returned to me when, on the even of war, the *Magpie* died an untimely death. However, with the manuscript came another personal letter from the editor, regretful, encouraging, and containing the suggestion that I should consider the theme afresh as the basis of a novel.

At this time I had read singularly few novels other than those of Dickens (then and now a passion of mine), Thackeray, Jane Austen, and Charlotte Brontë. (Charlotte was another of my passions !) Beyond a little Galsworthy and some cheap reprints of established writers like W. B. Maxwell and the now-neglected Elizabeth Robins, I had no acquaintance with contemporary fiction. The writing of a novel to a young woman engaged in earning a living and improving such shining hours as remained, who left the house at nine, and frequently did not return to it until ten, seemed a prodigious task, and I postponed a beginning until after my marriage in the middle of the war.

Working along the lines of the hint thrown out by the friendly and helpful *Magpie* editor, I found that my rejected story formed a strong thread in the fabric of the novel I had been turning over in my mind. It took me three years to write down, in the intervals of running a small house, cooking the meals, doing odd secretarial jobs, teaching shorthand to young women who wanted, with its aid, to rush out and seize lucrative Government posts while they were still to be had—and presently in visiting a husband stuck up on a bleak Lincolnshire plain with what was then the Royal Naval Air Force. Into this book went memories of my Puritanic upbringing, with its revivalist meetings and distrust of everything which seemed to me to make life worth living; my student days at my commercial school; a study of that famous publicist, Horatio Bottomley, for whom I worked for some years, and of his equally famous paper, *John Bull*; my passion for the open country, inherited from generations of country-bred forbears, and much of my pacifist attitude to the war which had cut my youth, as it had cut so many other people's, neatly in half. All these things emerged presently as *Invisible Tides*—a first novel which was as much a study of the war years seen by a young woman who hated them and stayed at home, as the story of two young people who met and loved, and suffered in them. When the war was over I sat down to a cold-blooded three months' revision of my manuscript and sent it to Mr. Arthur Waugh, of Chapman and Hall, who at once accepted it. So I found myself, in November 1919, actually launched as a novelist! About this initial effort nothing pleases me so much to remember now as the fact that, years later, when I came to know John Galsworthy, he told me that he had read and admired it!

Nevertheless, although I published novels steadily from that date to this, I have never been able entirely to resist the short story form around which my young ambitions were so fervently centred. Some part or thread of several of my novels has been written down as a short story—*Three Wives*, for example, *Youth Rides Out*, and *Maids and Mistresses*. The young servant-girl heroine in the last-named, who found so much favour in that and a subsequent volume, *Interlude for Sally*, had, in the first instance, a whole story to herself. But she made her bow to no editor. Her story was consigned immediately to the darkness of my desk drawer, where it remained until one fine day, four or five years later, when I took it out, re-read it, and bethought me that Sally would make an excellent chorus to a study of two post-war marriages I was contemplating. It is, therefore, perhaps true to say that although there has been rather a vogue of late for the servant heroine, Sally is entitled to consider herself as one of the earliest—if not *the* earliest— of them all.

Of the numerous short stories I have written since my teens, there are scarcely any which, at this time of day, are not to be regarded either as 'prentice work that I am grateful to Time for obliterating, or as detailed sketches for full-length novels. Of all that have been printed I could bear, I think, to re-read none of them, except perhaps *Journey's End*, which Mr. Arthur Waugh included in *Georgian Stories*, 1927—and even that, I feel now, I must have known to be only the final scene in a novel I would one day write.

Perhaps the short-story form cannot be used for such a purpose as the one I attempted to foist upon it. Growing up at a time when women were at their most clamorous for political and social recognition, it was only natural, I suppose, that I should have tried to use my story telling to re-state the relationships of men and women in the light of their altered mutual status. The short story, I am now convinced, cannot be used as a vehicle for social ideas ; the novel can. Perhaps that explains why I am a novelist when, from my youth upward, my intention was to win recognition for myself as a writer of short stories !

HELEN SIMPSON

I BEGAN to write to escape from failure in another art. This is not a bid for sympathy; the failure was deserved. My attempt upon the degree of Mus.Bac., Oxon., was made in order to gratify a natural uppishness and wish to be different. Proof that music itself meant and means very little to me is easily offered; during the past five years I have lived close to Queen's Hall, and have entered it perhaps half a dozen times.

I am able now, sixteen years after, to see as a stranger that young person who went up to Oxford in 1919. She wore, for economy partly, the dark blue uniform of the W.R.N.S., its brass buttons transmuted to non-committal black; this with an eyeglass. She was full of self-confidence; had intelligence, which thus far had only been put to the narrowest tests; and was consumed with a passion to be noticed and admired. All sorts of devices, some laughable, were pressed into this latter service. Even the monocle served its turn ; it became an insignia so personal that one astigmatic fresher who really needed a single glass was advised by her compeers to ask permission of Miss Simpson before she wore it. The permission was accorded. Miss Simpson ceremonially smashed her own glass against the mantelpiece that night, and never used one after.

What school was such a personage to take ? I had no mathematics, and could never have passed Responsions, to which sesame all the main schools opened. Without it only the Geography and French diplomas offered, or their even less distinguished opposite number, the diploma in Economics. I could not contemplate these. Ranging about among possibilities, I discovered that the Music School accepted candidates who could pass its own special Preliminary in English and two other languages. This I could manage. Lenient examiners passed me, and there I was, set up and swaggering as the only woman of my year taking the degree in music.

So far, good. Now came the uneasy realization that I was perfectly ignorant of everything save what Dr. Johnson called the alphabet of music, the clefs and the relationship of the notes. I could not play the piano properly, nor sing at sight. I had never seen an exercise in harmony in my life; the $\frac{5}{3}$ and $\frac{6}{4}$ symbols of a figured bass meant nothing whatever. I had no notion, even, of the compass of the human singing voice, let alone the capabilities of instruments. These were matters which the contrivers of the Music Prelim. did not attempt to ascertain concerning their candidates, rightly supposing that nobody would be such a fool as to tackle a difficult art without some grounding in its principles.

In one of Barrie's earlier books there is an incident which I may give here without irrelevance. Tommy, the poseur, pretends to have sprained his ankle; Grizel, the practical, sees through this pretence. He deliberately and privately bangs the door upon his foot, enduring the physical pain gladly as an alternative to confessing himself a sham.

I do not know how to convey the misery that must be undergone by a person who, wholly ignorant of music, and lacking any real love for it, pitches head-first into ten hours a day of it in order to gratify the instinct to show off. Aural training, for instance, the discipline which teaches immediate recognition of sounds and their relationship, could pervade the whole waking existence. You might hear at night a taxi hooting; A flat or A natural? It became necessary for your peace of mind to know. You slid out of bed and downstairs in the cold to the piano, carrying the horn note all the while in your head, and there softly, for fear of waking the house, tested your guess. The squeak of a shoe, the voice of a friend, the chink of a hammer—such sounds beset you and were at once translated, set down in black and white on a stave in your mind.

The written exercises were no easier. Often I could not tell what was expected of me when one was set; the guiding symbols were meaningless. I had to work out every bar with a piano, since I had no idea, during those first terms, how anything that I wrote would sound. Never once did the stuff I handed in look anything like other students' performances. Here comes the irony. I began to get a reputation for originality among my peers, who supposed that I simply would not be bothered with rules, while actually I was trying harder than any of them to be orthodox. I was in the position of a foreigner whose very unfamiliarity with the language he is using sometimes shows up an old idiom in a new light, and whose phrases make sense, though not always that which he thinks.

My tutor was not taken in. He never called me a fraud in so many words; indeed, he often, I believe, covered my ignorance from others. He may have suspected the truth, that I was putting in, to save my pride, a very great deal of hard work every day. But sometimes, nodding kindly over an exercise, he would say: "Yes, yes. But we have to think of the examiners; hide-bound fellows; their nerves won't stand much. And really, you know, some of these modulations of yours are very abrupt."

After a couple of terms I was beginning to get the hang of things, but still the patterns I made conveyed only their rhythm and tune correctly to my ear. Harmony baffled me. I could not then, and cannot now, contrive to hear clearly more than three parts moving at once. But in order to keep up that reputation for originality I had to show something now and then, and I hit, like the young man in the poem, on a strange device. I have wondered since that some one seeking an easy reputation has not developed it, and that I did not myself

make more of it. Briefly, it was music written
for the eye. You did landscapes, using the
black notes as trees ; demi-semiquavers, with
their many branches like lop-sided toy firs,
served well here in groups. In a song-series,
whose words were taken from Gautier's *Fan-
taisies d'Hiver*, I remember one line—" *les
pas étoilés des oiseaux* "—accompanied by trip-
lets which looked in fact very like the marks
of birds' feet. There were caricatures, done
in minims and crotchets, and one work entitled " The Drowned Man," whose accompani-
ment consisted solely of semibreves floating
from the bottom of the bass clef to the top of
the treble, like great bubbles ascending. This
nonsense I justified by copious quotations
from Gautier and his theory of the transposing
of arts. It went down well.

But such adventures in composition took
time, and though I enjoyed such *réclame* as they
brought me, I was not much nearer being a
genuine musician when they were down in
black and white ; I knew it perfectly well, and
was not bluffed by my own performances.
Even when my tutor played two of my piano
preludes at a public concert—goodness knows
why, except that they were diabolically difficult

and a challenge to virtuosity—I was not inwardly puffed up. It was the same feeling that I have had bringing off a preposterous bluff at poker, not so much pleased with myself as contemptuous of those who had allowed themselves to be taken in by me. But the months were passing; at the end of the academic year I was for it. Examiners would see through me. I knew that if I were set down with six ordinary questions in counterpoint to answer and no piano at my elbow I should simply make a fool of myself. I might have refused to sit for the first Mus.Bac. That would have been the honest course, but at this period I simply was not honest, and I could not bear the confession of failure that such a refusal implied. The only alternative—leaving aside such expedients as falling ill—was to fail deliberately, colossally, and with dash.

I began to plan for this two months before the examination. People all about me lamented their fate, wondered what class they would get. Amid this I alone was calm, mysteriously smiling, and intimating that I knew my fate already. " I shall plough." " What ? Why ? " " My dears, look at the people who are going to get through. Can't associate with them,

even on a Results form." In this way it got
about that I, through sheer impudence and for
the matter of a pose, was going not to try.
There was one bad moment when my tutor
suddenly said, having heard this rumour,
perhaps : " I hope you're taking this exam.
seriously. I don't like my people to fail."
This was hardly bearable, for I was fond of him,
but my idiot *amour-propre* could see no other
way out.

The papers, when I came to them at last,
were humane, not academic, set to give scope
to the candidate's imagination. The harmony
paper, for instance, gave four lines of verse,
and invited a setting for any combination of
instruments. I thought out some nonsensical
blend, bassoons and triangles, let us say—it
was not that, but I forget the exact absurdity—
handed in my paper at the end of twenty
minutes, and strolled out. The same with the
counterpoint questions ; I played the fool with
them for twenty minutes, and wandered off
to spend the rest of the afternoon in a punt.
When the time came for the Viva, the examination by word of mouth, three beautifully robed
gentlemen looked at me narrowly, and with
great politeness asked me to tell them what

harmonic series was to be obtained from the seventh position on the trombone. I knew this, and gave the answer correctly in order to puzzle them, and to show that my fooling with the questions on paper had been intentional. They let me go almost at once.

On the day when results were to be known I did not go near the Schools. " Oh, don't be so maddening ! You must want to know ! " " I do know. I've ploughed, as I had every intention of doing, and now I can get on with my novel in peace." "Novel ! When on earth did you start thinking of that ? " " About the beginning of this term, so I chucked the Mus.Bac. to get on with it." " How much have you done ? When will it be finished ? " " In three weeks."

I had not written a word of it. I had no plot, and no more notion of writing English than, a year back, I had had of music. But words, after all, are the omnibus in which we make our daily journeys of the mind, and I felt that I could string enough of them together to bear out my boast. I took the first plot that came to hand, therefore, and during three weeks of rain at St. Jean de Luz laboured at this self-imposed job. It was easy. It was simply giving body to the stories I was accustomed to tell myself to keep away fear of the dark. The actual writing out by hand of sixty-five thousand words is no light task, but my imagination endured none of the appalling blanknesses that had been used to come upon it when it roved in the unfamiliar fields of regimented sound. I was sorry when, on the last day of that rainy month, the story was done. Whether it was good or bad stuff of its kind I did not then know, but I despised it, I remember, for coming so easily ; not having as yet enough experience of life to understand that, as Samuel Butler points out, most of the things an individual does best he does effortlessly, in a way that runs with, and not against, the grain of his aptitudes.

The book in typescript, my second flight from reality began to take something the curve of the first. For it was no good boasting that I had written a novel if there were to be nothing to show ; print was the only proof of my feat worth offering. So there I was, on the horns of the same dilemma, with publishers' readers substituted for my previous board of examiners. But now there was this in my favour, that while an examiner's opinion must be made public, a publisher's need not ; nor is one publisher's

" No " binding upon all his fellows. I asked advice, and followed this by sending the script to Heinemann's. But among my friends I used the same tactics that before had spared me humiliation; deprecating the book, insisting that it would not be taken, that I had sent it in for a bet and so on. Mr. C. S. Evans has told me since that at one of the cocktail parties of the period his host greeted him : " I say, d'you know Helen Simpson ? " " Never heard of her." " Well, anyway, she says she's just sent you in a damn bad book."

All these precautions of mine, these forestallings and mockings of failure, as it happened, served no purpose. The novel was taken, and I don't know that I have ever been more surprised in my life. But it was not the sort of contemptuous surprise I had felt when my musical extravagances were accepted at Oxford. I knew that those were shams pure and simple. This book at least was written in English as good as I could manage, the plot was dramatic, and the people seemed to me not incredible. When the reviews came out, taking it seriously, I was not ashamed as when my tutor played in public those two tortuous preludes. What I had written during those wet weeks in France did at least make sense, if it had cost no effort.

This gave me to think. The novel had been so quickly performed that I had no recollection of how any of my effects were brought off. All the same, I knew that they had not been flukes ; some kind of artistic conscience or consciousness had acted as censor, and might do so again. I set to work, very cautiously, on some short stories, testing my way in this new art as though I were walking among quicksands ; but all the while—and this I realized by the time that second book was completed—my feet were on firm ground. That is not to say I enjoyed reading the stuff I wrote. I believe this to be the particular cross of writers, and one that is not laid upon the shoulders of other artists : that often they write in a manner, and of events or people, which would repel them in a book picked up by chance in a library. An artist paints, I suppose, the pictures he wants to paint ; that is, supposing him free from economic pressure. But I have found surprisingly few writers who admit to enjoying their own kind of books, which looks as though we should dislike our subconscious selves very heartily if our souls were suddenly to turn bottom upwards.

This knowledge, that my subconscious self is waiting somewhere in the deeps or shallows of my soul to give me the lie, acts now as a check upon confession. I should like to say that since I have found something I can do, which brings in money and causes me to be noticed in the newspapers, I have become honest; that is, I no longer catch myself out in lies, because there is no longer any special reason for me to cheat myself and others, or to pose. But it may not be so; I will not be absolute about it. " What dreams may come," as Hamlet said, anticipating Freud, " must give us pause," and it may be only that I have become more wily, better able to deceive myself; proof that my mind is a sink of iniquity may be found, by those who understand such things, in the admission that I no longer have dreams.

I do, however, know two things for sure: it gives me pleasure to weigh, to use, and even to write words; and it has given me neither shame nor satisfaction to display here the expedients to which I was put sixteen years ago. Those terms at Oxford simply stand for a time of experiment, the necessary elbow-room that individuals need who grow up late. They were painful, but they left no trace, and I can speak of them as dispassionately as of the mumps which came my way during 1919. You must be a fool at some time of your life, just as before you die you must eat a peck of dirt. Now I believe that I am wiser ; I know that I am happier. And not for all the tea in China would I be eighteen again.

L. A. G. STRONG

I WONDER how many children know, almost from the beginning of their conscious lives, certain cardinal facts about their future. In my own case, three or four of the most important things that have happened to me I had so confidently anticipated from early childhood that, when in due course they came, I greeted them with recognition and without surprise. To mention a couple of them would be outside our present business; but I had calmly accepted, from the time I was four or five, the fact that I should one day go to Oxford, although nothing could have then seemed more unlikely. Not only were our circumstances such as to make a university out of the question, but my father did not approve of public schools or of universities as places of education. This, however, did not trouble me. The avenue that led to our home at Plymouth was called Oxford Avenue; I knew that I should one day go to Oxford. In the same way, although my only immediate talent was for drawing, I knew that I should one day write.

I was born on the 8th of March 1896, in the parish of Plympton, in Devon. My father is half West Country English and half Connaught Irish, my mother altogether Irish, from Dublin and the north. This mongrelism, with the results it was to bring about, served me well. I was taken to Hampstead for a time, when I was too young to remember anything about it ; spent a winter with my grandparents in Kingstown, and rejoined my parents in the first home I can remember—Mutley Park House, Plymouth. In 1902 my father had an illness, and was sent out to Dousland, on the fringe of the moor, to recuperate. The air proved so beneficial that, a year later, we all moved out to Yelverton, and remained there for fifteen years.

Every summer we went over to my grandparents in Kingstown. I became obstreperous, and wanted to fish off the sea-wall. A younger sister took up most of the nurse's time, and so my grandmother hired a lame fisherman to initiate me into the craft, and look after me generally. With this good friend, who appears in more than one of my books under his own name, I entered into the lives of the people along the sea front at an age when one is content simply to accept experience. What I learned then has been of incalculable value to me, all the more so because I did not realize that I was learning anything. At home, too, I spent a year at a tiny local school, and, likewise without knowing it, learned the ways of an entirely different race, the country folk of Devon. As a result, I am literally and mentally bilingual : that is to say, I can speak Devon dialect and Dublin Irish well enough to be accepted as native to either place, and I can think quite naturally and without effort in the terms of both. Dialects interest me, and I have acquired several others since, through mimicry, but nothing can take the place of that early unconscious absorption which makes a thing instinctive.

My first attempts at writing were brief celebrations of the lives of woodlice, caterpillars, fleas, and such like, of which none survive. Then came a poem, of which I can remember only the single line, " Alcides was an ass." The next I remember very well indeed. Belonging to preparatory schooldays, it was a long and exceedingly moral ballad, in so-called Chaucerian language, entitled, " Amelia, ye aged sow." It described, with much gusto and in considerable detail, the fate which befell two small boys who persecuted Amelia with an airgun. The theme, I regret to say, was suggested by the malpractice of a friend and myself, who, on more than one occasion, took pot shots at the largest sow on a farm of which we enjoyed the run. This ballad (it was recently published in its original form) caused something of a stir in the family, not because of its precocity, but because Amelia was the name of my Irish grandmother. I protested with tears that no disrespect was intended, for I worshipped my Granny, but that I had used the name Amelia simply because it was the perfect name for the sow in question, whose outlook on life and whose demise alike seemed to accord with the best-accepted tenets of Victorian morality.

The preparatory school, now, alas, no more, did me a lot of good. There taught at it a lady with a real enthusiasm for literature, Miss Cherrill, now headmistress of a flourishing preparatory school at Bude. Hers was the only sort of English teaching that matters, the sort which makes a pupil want to explore for himself. The rest of the teaching was good of its kind, though erratic, owing to frequent changes in the staff; but hers stood out. We read Shakespeare in class, and enjoyed it. When, in 1907, my father first took me to London, I chose for my theatre treat a visit to *The Merchant of Venice* at His Majesty's. Tree was the Shylock, Basil Gill the Bassanio, and Alexandra Carlisle the Portia. I was enthralled, but critical; and I remember discussing with Miss Cherrill, when I got back, Tree's rendering, and the elaborate business he interpolated into the text. It was a good English class where, in 1907, an hour could be spent discussing, with imitations, the respective renderings of a part by Tree and Irving, while the rest of the class looked on.

Not that my reading consisted entirely of the classics. With the friend who helped me persecute Amelia, I was a gluttonous devourer of penny dreadfuls. That was the Augustan age of the penny dreadful: the bookstalls of to-day can show nothing like it. The *Dick Turpin Library*, the *Robin Hood Library*, the *Buffalo Bill Library* were going strong, to the tune of four numbers a month; the *Claud Duval Library* was still obtainable, and, by hunting about, one could still purchase odd numbers of the *Jack Sheppard Library*. We read them all, together with the *Gem* and the *Magnet* (Tom Merry, Harry Wharton, and Billy Bunter are happily still with us), and the *Marvel*, featuring Jack, Sam, and Pete. In addition to these, there were the comic papers : *Puck*, with the Newlyweds and Professor Radium ; *Comic Cuts*, with Gertie, the regimental mule ; and *Lot o' Fun*, with Dreamy Daniel. On higher levels there were the *Boys' Own Paper* and *The Captain*, in which Mr. P. G. Wodehouse was establishing himself with a series of the best school stories that have ever been written. It was the best of all times to be a boy.

One day, my friend Arthur Rodd and I decided that we would write a penny dreadful for ourselves. Of the many available heroes we chose Buffalo Bill. I wish I had the result. The interesting thing about it was that it was a parody. We realized the absurdity of some of these stories, and made our own much more absurd, half in a spirit of parody, but half because we enjoyed revelling in an even more preposterous bloodshed than the original. At one point, finding the work heavy, we co-opted a third collaborator, only to dismiss him in disgrace after he had written a single paragraph;

not because his stuff lacked spirit, but because he could not spell. This, for some reason, offended our sense of propriety.

My last year at the Hoe Preparatory School was too much taken up with working for a scholarship for any more literary endeavours. I won the scholarship, and went to Brighton College. There I found drawing a quick road to popularity, and began to work at it. During a cross-country run, in my second term, I overtaxed my strength in some way, and laid the foundation for a weakness which was to last for several years and keep me out of the war. I spent three months on my back at home, drawing, and reading Dickens, and all the minor Elizabethan dramatists on whom I could lay my hands. I did not return to Brighton till the following January. Instead, as soon as I was well enough, I went back as a boarder to my preparatory school, where one of the assistant masters, Cecil Glenn, an eccentric genius who was later killed in the war, acted as my tutor. His instruction was sound, if unorthodox, and I owe a great deal to him. It included, among other things, experiments in telepathy and table-turning. These became alarmingly successful, and we

164

only abandoned them because they used to leave us with such violent headaches on the day following.

One week of this autumn term was spent in visiting every performance of the Benson Shakespearian Company at the Theatre Royal. I read each play during the day, and saw it in the evening. What a company it was! Benson, Ellen O'Malley (the best Juliet I have ever seen), Ethel McDowall, Randle Ayrton, Murray Carrington, Moffat Johnston, Henry Caine, Dennis Neilson - Terry, fresh from Charterhouse—all gave performances which I shall never forget. Other experiences included visits to various Plymouth clubs and queerer haunts, a considerable insight into the lives of my elders (Glenn was completely candid about himself and others), and a nocturnal vigil with plain-clothes police officers from a bedroom window upon a suspected house of ill-fame. Besides all this, Glenn gave a great fillip to my writing ambitions. Whenever he was hard up, which was about every three weeks, he would dash off three or four newspaper articles, written anyhow, in pencil, on the backs of old exercises, and post them off. They were invariably accepted, and, cashing his cheques, he would jingle a handful of sovereigns in front of my nose and take me off with him to pay the more pressing of his debts.

When I got back to Brighton, drawing was still uppermost, and I did no more writing till I was seventeen. Then, influenced by a friend, Vincent Morris, one of the many poets whose lives were to be cut short on the battlefield, I began to write verses. Several of the poems in *Dublin Days* belong to this time. I was rather ashamed of these, regarding them as an infection from my Dublin holidays, and from the Abbey Theatre, which I had rapturously discovered in 1912; and much preferred Tennysonian imitations, of an incredible badness, which I wrote fluently. Vincent and I agreed that these were " poetry," whereas my uncouth, vernacular rhymes could be nothing of the sort. During these last two years I entered upon another collaboration, the fruit of which, likewise, has not survived. This time my collaborator was G. B. Harrison, now the celebrated Shakespearian scholar. There is at Brighton College a bell tower, containing a spiral staircase which leads up to the bell loft. Rising from beside the porter's lodge, it has a small window opening upon what then was the headmaster's study, and a door, partly hidden by the master's dais and desk, which gave access to it from the classroom above the study. This door, contrary to expectation, was unlocked, and Harrison and I clambered in one day and explored. The place, we noted, offered numerous diversions. That of climbing up and interfering with the bells we dismissed at once, for Harrison was a prefect of standing, and I had just been made one. The window looking down into the headmaster's study was more promising, but perilous, for the headmaster was not a man to be trifled with. He had, however, a secretary, who in turn had a dog. This dog, a large and ferocious beast, would sometimes be left alone in the study, when the headmaster and his secretary were engaged elsewhere. The window was many feet above the ground, and amusement could be had by making noises through it and exciting the dog. When properly roused, the animal would rush at and attempt to bite the first person to enter the room; and on one memorable occasion we did our work so thoroughly that it bit its master.

However, this had nothing to do with our collaboration, which concerned an apocryphal

monster, supposed to haunt the tower. First
of all, we decided to work up a little local
interest. With an old fives glove and some
luminous paint we printed three-toed footprints upon the walls of the tower. We
secreted ourselves there at odd times, and I,
who had the knack of uttering sepulchral and
inhuman guffaws, frightened the man who was
cleaning the classroom almost into a fit by
letting one off close beneath his feet. Deeply
satisfactory, more flattering than any shriek of
terror, was the instant of horrified silence, then
the clatter of pan and brush as the poor man
took to his heels. The pair of us instantly
emerged, got safely out of the classroom door,
and were strolling down the passage when we
met him, whitefaced and shaking, wondering
if he dare go back.

We did our best after this to spread the
legend, and people went and gazed in awe at
the luminous footprints; but the difficulty of
providing further phenomena checked us, and
somehow neither the fabrication nor the story
got beyond its opening chapters. Then Harrison, who was my senior, left for Cambridge,
and I began working for a scholarship to
Oxford. I had just managed to get myself

transferred from the Modern to the Classical side, and was faced with the difficulty of learning in just over two years enough Greek to get by the examiners. I made the fateful journey to Oxford in 1914, and, a week later, was put out of my misery by reading my name on the notice board at Wadham.

Before going into residence I had been examined medically for a commission in the army or the navy, and rejected by both. I came up to an Oxford which was not even a travesty of the real thing. The colleges, inhabited by those not able-bodied enough to be elsewhere, were soon to be barracks for cadets. To work was difficult, almost impossible. Not all the undergraduates were crocks ; there were a few conscientious objectors, and, of course, the American Rhodes Scholars. The attitude of the general public was pitying, contemptuous, or definitely hostile. " Only a few more days," people would call after us in the streets, and I own that I was glad when the Derby scheme enabled me to wear an armlet and prove that I was entitled to be where I was.

The circumstances, driving us all in upon ourselves, sent each man to his appropriate emotional outlet. I began writing hard. A handful of the Dublin verses, sent in to the *'Varsity*, procured me a visit from the editor, Russell Green. He took me to Beaumont Street, where T. W. Earp held court, and in those hospitable rooms, which meant more to many of us then than we shall ever be able to say, I met Aldous Huxley, Robert Nichols, Wilfred Childe, and many another. We all wrote, and, once a week, used to meet and produce what we had written. Discussion and criticism were often vigorous, but the most dramatic comment I remember was unspoken. A poem of Robert Nichols produced such a violent effect upon Wilfred Childe that he fainted.

As the months went by the band grew thinner. Soon Robert Graves, recovering from a severe wound, arrived at Wadham, in charge of cadets. My first meeting with him arose from a projected raid by his charges upon a coloured undergraduate. In 1917, unwell and unable to get on with my work, I obtained leave to replace a man in a civilian post. The first vacancy was at Summer Fields, the famous Oxford Preparatory School. I went for an interview, was accepted, and stayed for two years, returning at the end of that time to finish my academically inglorious career. By this time I was really ill again, and spent some of that last year in a bath chair. It was a happy year, all the same, for Oxford was alive again, and full of poets and writers. There were in residence Graves, Edmund Blunden (whom I had first met on the cricket field at Brighton, playing against us for Christ's Hospital), William Force Stead, Louis Golding, Alan Porter, and many others. A. E. Coppard was about the place, Edward O'Brien lived at Forest Hill, and at his house I used to meet John Cournos, and, later, Romer Wilson. Sir Walter Raleigh presided over the English school. It was a glorious time. Like every one else, I wrote abundantly —too abundantly, as the following skit by Louis Golding suggests. The name he chose for me was painfully appropriate, as, owing to want of exercise, I had lost my figure!

PASTORAL

By Leonard Stout

Little Leonard, tricksy youth
(I'se afeard you'll not believe
As I'm tellin' the 'ole truth),
Wipes ees nose upon ees sleeve.

171

Eena meena mina mo !
After mixin' of ees wines,
Leonard, standin' on ees toe,
Spits upon the railway lines.

O it's dimpsey on the watter !
If yer wants brand-new effects—
Dublin, Devon, it don't matter—
Just combine the dialects.

Don't yer find the thought entices
For to be the Muses' votary ?—
Weekly splendour in the "Isis,"
Canonization in the "Coterie" !

Eena meena mina meena !
Aldous Huxley, Russel Greena,
Wyndham Lewis, Nina Hamnett,
    Baa—baa—baa,
      Damn ett !

In September 1920 I went back to Summer
Fields. My first book of verses, *Dublin Days*,
appeared just a year later. Mr. W. B. Yeats
had come to live in Oxford, and I dared to send
him a copy. A few days later came a letter,
difficult to read but well worth the effort,
saying nice things about the book and asking
me to go and see him. For the next two years
I visited him regularly, and learned more than
at any other period in my life. His kindness

and encouragement, coming at a time when I was in every way unstable, were of incalculable value. These evenings set me on my feet, both mentally and physically.

I now became very self-critical, writing much less, and destroying more than half I wrote. In 1921 I first began regularly to submit my work to editors. The first twelve months brought me in a few shillings over thirty pounds. Six years afterwards, when I had been two years married, I was still earning less than a hundred a year from writing. *Doyle's Rock*, my first volume of short stories, appeared in 1925. It was very unequal, had some success with the critics, and sold badly. In 1929 my first novel, *Dewer Rides*, after being turned down by one publisher, was accepted and published by Gollancz. Originally planned as a poem, it had taken, in all, about two years to write. Schoolmasters need most of their holidays to recover from the physical stress of term, and, during term, the only time I could find for writing was, at the most, an hour a day, and that usually before breakfast.

After this, my life as a writer had fairly begun. All sorts of surprising things happened. Editors began to take an interest in me. Stories which had hitherto been rejected were accepted, sometimes by the very journals that had rejected them. What was even more surprising, I began to receive commissions, and there is nothing so stimulating as an order for a piece of work unseen. A commission will often provoke a writer's best work : it is a challenge, a tonic ; it suggests to him an idea he did not possess ; it enables him suddenly to make use of one he did possess, and, to some natures more important than all, it proves to him that a business man is ready to back his opinion with hard cash.

Encouraged by all this, I hurried to write a second novel, *The Jealous Ghost*. My publisher was dubious. I offered to withdraw it. He would not accept the offer. I wish he had !

Now came a real cross-roads. I was getting far too much to do. Schoolmastering does not leave one much spare time, and by the evening, when most spare-time writers do their work, I was always too tired for writing. Clearly, I had to choose between my two jobs. It was a case of trying to do one well, or doing both badly. Timid and conservative, I hesitated ; then, with real regret, resigned my post at Summer Fields. That last summer term I shall never forget. I was working at a rate one could not keep up for long—a new novel, *The Garden*, for an hour before breakfast ; a book of criticism, *Common Sense About Poetry*, for an hour after breakfast ; then my day's work at school, and all sorts of odd writing jobs, articles, a short story or two, and my first efforts at reviewing fiction for *The Spectator*. In spite of all this, I enjoyed every minute of the term. We went off to Scotland for a long holiday, remained there till October, and came back to our flat at Oxford to clear things up for our departure. There, as soon as I had learned not to jump up when the school bell rang, I finished *The Garden*. In November we packed up, said our good-byes, and migrated to two furnished rooms in Pimlico. I was a writer at last !

ALEC WAUGH

THE first novelist I ever knew gave me this advice : " Don't write novels about novelists." At least I thought then that he was giving me advice. I have realized since that he was stating an axiom.

Every novelist draws up for himself a list of rules—a list of " Don'ts " for the most part. Each list is different. But there is one entry that will appear in every list : " Don't write novels about novelists." Sooner or later, of course, the rule is broken, to be regretted almost invariably. A curious atmosphere of unreality will envelop the entire story. The hero will never seem quite human. The novelist leads a more varied life than most men who depend for their livelihood on their own exertions. He can work where he likes, when he likes, under conditions of his own choosing. The circumference of his life is drawn by the radius of his interests. Yet he is only a profitable subject when he is the mythical " I," the

narrator, the figure in the background. I
cannot think of a single convincing novelist
" hero " anywhere in fiction.

The explanation, it seems to me, is this.
Work, to the man who is worth anything, is
his life. It is by the success or failure of his
work that he sits in judgment on himself. His
personal, private life, though not exactly a side-
show, is seen in relation to his work : as a help
or hindrance ; as the particular conditions that
have obstructed, redirected, or inspired his
ambition. The measure of a man's interest to
his fellows is the extent and nature of his
achievement. It is equally by the extent and
nature of that achievement that the interest of
his private life is measured. Mary Fytton is
of importance and significance because her
lover wrote *King Lear* ; Lady Hamilton because
Nelson was the hero of Trafalgar. It is one of
the dramatist's axioms that the hero of a tragedy
must be himself heroic. Nero, for example, is
not a fit subject for a tragedy.

The point I am trying to make is this : that
since no man without a career or without inherited or acquired responsibilities—that is to
say, the equivalent for a career—is a suitable
hero for a novel, the novelist, if he is to make

a male character convincing, has got to convince the reader of the reality of the " career-problems " that the hero has to face. He has to show a man fighting for his position in the world, to achieve the things on which his heart is set. He has to explain the points at which courage, resolution, skill are needed to control the issue. When the novelist has done that, then he has created a character in whose love affairs and domestic trials he can reasonably expect the reader to take an interest.

Which is the reason why it is so extremely difficult, why it is almost impossible, to make a novelist the hero of a novel. Impossible because his work side, his most essential side, cannot be effectively presented. The conflict takes place entirely in the novelist's own mind. His problems are of his own making, and for his own solution. They are intangible and undramatic. There is no moment of crisis that could be transported to the stage. His work is done in the privacy of a study. He is concerned with difficulties of technique and style that involve no personal relations. His interviews with publishers and editors are, thanks to the diplomacy of his agent, of a more or less social nature. He has none of the dramatic issues that confront the manipulator of stocks and companies ; there are no directors to be conciliated, exposed, or shouldered out of office. He has not, as the statesman, to cajole or override refractory cabinets. He is not opposed, as the explorer is, by hostile elements. He has no moments of gesture ; no real moments, for that matter, of success or failure. There is no equivalent for the dramatist's speech to a cheering first-night audience. Indeed, not until the book has been several weeks upon the market is he in a position to judge the exact nature of its reception—by the public and the critics. Flaubert's picture of himself seated at a window in a dressing-gown watching the Seine flow past, waiting for the inevitable word, is a caricature of the average novelist, but like every good caricature the resemblance to the original is recognizably apparent.

The work side of a novelist's life provides the novelist with the minimum of material. Nor, curiously enough, does his personal life provide really satisfactory " copy." For though the novelist's personal life is so interknit with his writing life that the one may be said to feed the other—so that his personal life is not so much a harbour where he can relax and be restored, as the raw material for his writing ; though, indeed, that personal life, owing to greater leisure and freedom of movement, is more likely to be filled with incident than is the average man's, even so the basic problem of that personal life is in the last analysis an impersonal one. A novelist is not so much coping with a series of personal relationships as setting himself the question, " How am I to arrange my personal life to the most effective service of my work ? " And that is another conflict to be staged in his own mind.

That problem is the framework by which his life is shaped. At the start it is very largely an arithmetical affair of hours and minutes : the problem, at a period when the unaided resources of his pen are insufficient for his self-support, of how he is to write novels in his spare time. Later, when he is freed from the routine of an office desk—the decision to rely wholly upon his pen is the one really dramatic step in a novelist's career—it is a final burning of boats—the problem still remains. For he has so to organize his life that he is in touch with the action of his day, yet has the tranquillity in which to think and write. It is not easy. It is a problem whose solution demands skill, ingenuity, perception, and a rather ruthless selfishness. Yet, since it is a problem whose episodes are set in the novelist's own mind, it is essentially undramatic.

In final fact, the essence of a novelist's life could only be effectively presented in a completely subjective novel that would be dull after twenty pages, and unreadable after forty.

It is for this reason that a novelist's story of " How I Began " must, of necessity, be less interesting than a barrister's, a soldier's, an explorer's. Myself, I have led and am leading a varied and amusing life. I have seen a good deal of the world. I have had as much glamour, adventure, excitement as the other man. When I have meditated suicide it is because I have been unhappy, not because I have been bored. Regarding myself as the observer and commentator, I have enough material for a two-volume autobiography. Yet I do not feel that I could write twenty readable pages under the title *Myself as a Novelist*, even though I am convinced that a writer is provided with just as many opportunities for displaying " a stiff upper lip " as the financier or surgeon, and though I hope and believe that I could write three hundred readable pages about a man

whose " early struggles " have been no more sub-
jected than mine to the vicissitudes of fortune.

I am the more convinced of this because my
friends, with one exception, refuse to believe
that I have ever had any " early struggles."

In their opinion I went in to bat on a pretty
easy wicket. Perhaps I did. I was spared,
anyhow, the typical difficulties of my craft.
There was no family opposition to contend with.
On the contrary, I had my father's encouragement and advice ; and that debt is so great
that it would be idle to attempt any assessment
of it. I was unendowed, to the extent that
from the age of eighteen I have had to earn every
penny that I have spent ; but I inherited that
for which most young writers would mortgage
large blocks of consols—a seat upon the board
of a publishing house of long traditions. Nor
did I have to wait for notice. Within a few
days of my nineteenth birthday my first novel
was proving itself to be the second best-seller of
1917. (*Sonia* was the first.) If you look at
it from one point of view, I had no early
struggles whatsoever. I prefer to look at it
from another : to say that my difficult time
came after, instead of before, the publication
of my first book.

This was the position in which I found myself when I left the army in the Christmas of 1918. I was twenty and a half. *The Loom of Youth* was selling steadily. My name was more often than not included in articles on "The Younger Novelists." Magazines and newspapers were anxious for my work. A literary advisorship to Chapman and Hall was waiting for me. The ball was apparently at my feet. Perhaps it was. But I knew very well that I had neither the ability nor the strength to kick it.

I had spent the last eight months of the war in a German prison camp. I had been afforded, that is to say, a pretty good opportunity for stocktaking. I had also been brought into touch, for the first time, with men considerably older than myself. In particular with Gerard Hopkins and Hugh Kingsmill (*neé* Lunn). They gave me friendship and advice. By the time I came back to England I had realized two things : the first, that whatever my next novels were like, I should be told that they were poor stuff, and that I was clearly *homo unius libri* ; the second, which was far more important, that I stood little chance of writing anything worth reading for a considerable time, since not only had I learnt very little of the technique of writing, but knew hardly anything about adult life, and nothing at all of the world except under war-time conditions.

My job, that is to say, was to see something of the world, and to teach myself how to write.

As I said earlier, it is very hard to make a novelist's difficulties convincing. Perhaps it would be simplest if I were to take a simile from the cricket field. I felt during the six years after the war as a batsman does when the light is bad, the wicket difficult, and his eye is out. He says, " It is no good my attempting to hit boundaries. One mistake, and it is all over. I must just stay here, and keep my end up somehow. If I can do that, the wicket will in time get easier, the light will clear, I shall get a sight of the ball. But till then I must just stick here, not let the bowlers know they are on top, and snatch such singles as I can."

It was in that spirit that, after the war, I set myself to the writing of novels that wisely never left my desk, short stories that editors wisely returned to me, and newspaper articles that I may call the equivalent of snatched singles. I relied for money almost entirely upon articles.

I think it was easier for a writer to earn

money then than it is now : or rather, it was easier to earn a little. There is more big money to be made to-day ; a best-selling novel sells more copies, and " starred " articles are more highly paid. But in 1920 there were better openings for free-lance literary journalism. There were more newspapers ; there were fewer starred articles, and more space for the short essay. I do not think there is any such space to-day. It was not particularly well-paid work—two to three guineas a thousand was the average rate ; it was signed, and had to be done carefully. But it was there to be had. Which I do not think it is to-day. I do not believe that if I were to find myself now in the position that I was in in 1919 I should be able to pick up by free-lance journalism the two hundred or so pounds a year that supplemented the four pounds a week that Chapman and Hall paid me. I think I was lucky to have been born when I was.

But luck or no luck, it was not an easy time. I did not want to be a publisher. I did not want to be a journalist. I wanted to write novels and short stories. But I knew very well that the publication of three or four really poor novels would torpedo my reputation, very likely beyond repair. During those years I tore up at least half of what I wrote : two and a half novels, and heaven only knows how many short stories. I work fast. My job at Chapman and Hall's was a half-time one. I wrote during most of my spare time in the winter. But though I had finished *The Loom of Youth* in the spring of 1916, it was not till 1922 that I delivered my second novel to a publisher. And it was 1924 before I sold a short story to one of the big magazines.

In retrospect four or five years does not seem a long time. It seemed a long time then. For me it was dramatic. For me it was exciting. For me it was a battle. But there is nothing to show for it, since it was a battle waged in my own mind. I said to myself, " If I go on writing, but not publishing ; if I read carefully the novels I have most admired, discovering how the effects that moved me were produced, sooner or later I shall get some idea what it is about," or rather, what I was myself about ; for I did not know the kind of book I wanted to write any more than a débutante knows what kind of woman she wants to be ; what kind of person she is. She looks at herself in the glass. " Who am I ? What am I ? " she asks herself,

waiting for the moment that will reveal her to
herself.

I think most writers have a sensation very
much like this. They are puzzled. They are
self-conscious. They do not feel they are
getting themselves upon the paper. And then,
suddenly, without warning, a moment comes
and they are at ease. They are writing naturally ; they surrender to the rhythm of their
mood ; they have found themselves. Be their
talent great or little, they do what they have to
do without self-consciousness, speaking their
own thoughts out of their own natures, with
their own accents. For better or worse, they
have begun to exist as writers.

Most writers that I have talked to of this tell
me that they have had some such experience.
For me it came half-way through *Card Castle*,
my third novel. I had written, re-written, torn
up most of the first half of it through twenty
vacillating months. I had imagined that it was
destined to be another of my unpublished
novels. But suddenly, half-way through, I
found myself telling a story easily, with a
gathering excitement, with a sense of climax,
with a foreknowledge of the end.

Card Castle is a poorish novel. For the first

hundred pages, anyhow. And it met the fate that is reserved for novels that do not attract the reader's attention in the first ten minutes. It sold less than two thousand copies. No American publisher would handle it. On the literary bourse my stock touched new low-levels. Kindly intentioned friends suggested that Chapman and Hall really needed gingering up, and wouldn't I be wise to make a whole-time job of it ? " It'll interfere with your writing a bit, of course, but a lot of the best novels have been written in a man's spare time."

I was grateful to them for their tact. But for the first time for six years I was not worrying. I knew the excited glow of the batsman who feels that at last he is getting the pace of the wicket and a sight of the ball.

I thought, " I really can begin."

MALACHI WHITAKER

WHEN I saw downs for the first time they were familiar to me because of a cricket field I frequented at the age of four. This was only a small field. The pitch was in a hollow, and a grassy bank rolled gently up from it, to be crowned at the summit by a couple of eastward-bowing sycamore trees.

It was under one of these trees that I composed my first poem, ran home intoxicated across the cricket pitch, through a game in progress, stammered it breathlessly to my father, was given sixpence, and spent it, all within an hour. And almost thirty years later the same thing repeated itself in a more dignified fashion, with an editor in place of a father.

I live now within a few yards of that cricket field. The trees are cut down. A road runs through part of it, but I can still see it in its young-century beauty, feel the early summer warmth, know again the glory of the sun and the daisy that provoked the poem; because at that very moment (I could already read and write, being the eighth of a family of eleven) I became aware that I was in a marvellous place, that I was alive, and that I must say so.

My second poem was not so good. What I really wanted was another sixpence. I repeated my poem, which had given me a lot of trouble, but my father merely said, " You're too late, lass. Shakespeare said this first, and much better," and kept his hand in his pocket. So I went and pulled out a loose tooth—we got a penny for things like that—and thought a lot.

Afterwards, when I wrote anything, I would look at it for a long time, grow certain that somebody else had done it better, and tear it up. Anyhow, reading was so much pleasanter. I learned how to be deliberately naughty (I got noise of the ear-splitting kind into a fine art) so that I could be sent to bed where I could read in ecstasy, alone, and not have to look after one or more of my three little brothers.

Luckily for me my father was a bookbinder, so there were always plenty of books. Sometimes people would leave books at his place to bind, and forget to return for them. They were put in an attic, and so was I. It is hard to remember the names of all of them. There was *David*

Copperfield—though for many years I never got beyond page forty of him—*Wuthering Heights*, volume after volume of the *Family Herald Supplement*, *Tom Jones*, *Peregrine Pickle*, bound copies of *Tit-Bits*, *All the Year Round*, and *To-day*, *Les Misérables* (how I ploughed through that one), *Andersen's Fairy Tales*, *Vanity Fair*, and an old Bible.

The ones I could not read were *Don Quixote* and *Jessica's First Prayer*. There was a *Child's Bible* which I tried, but did not find suitable after the real one. I would look for words like hell and devil in the real Bible, and simply go on reading because I liked the rolling sound of the sentences. At my first school I got every Scripture prize going. There was also a book called *Little Meg's Children*, which delighted me at an early age. In that, or another very much like it, there were the words " Perseverance, paint, and glue, Eighteen hundred and eighty-two." I thought it a better poem than any of mine. And I was right.

At my second school I was a nasty child. I hated it so much, and was so miserable that I was forced to make a world of my own to get along at all. There was a three-mile walk to it, and that I enjoyed, summer and winter. There was so much to see, so much to do and think about. One of my favourite pursuits was following streams. If they went underground, so did I. But all I got was cold and dirty ; I got torn clothes and smackings, too ; and atmosphere.

There were no prizes, and no good marks of any kind for me at this school. I did my worst work at examinations, not from nervousness, but from contempt. And the whole of the time I was steadily writing and burning everything I wrote. Only once did I betray myself. We were told to write a story, and mine was read in front of the class. Feeble as it was, it was apparently the best of the lot. I was in an agony of shame. I remember telling the other girls that I had copied it out of a book. Somebody told the form-mistress, and she kept me behind and asked me why I was such a liar. I don't know what I said. All I wanted to do was get away.

About that time I read a story about a child who formed his letters so crookedly that one night they came out of the book, dragging themselves lamely in front of him, wanting to be made straight. That is what my own sentences still do. For a long time after my first book was published I used to wake in the night while badly expressed and broken paragraphs crept in chains of horror before my eyes. But I am trying to learn tolerance.

The war came then. Still determined to be a poet, I made up a set of windy martial verses, and sold them to a Christmas card firm for seven and sixpence. At the same time I was working twelve hours a day for from ten to twelve shillings a week. I use that as my excuse. Printed for some reason in mauve ink, these verses had the look of weak cocoa.

At the age of twenty I wrote my autobiography in fifty thousand words. I still have it. It amazes me by its arrogance. All I was not I put in that autobiography. Then I got married and went to live in France. And there I wrote a business novel, which, fortunately, fell overboard from a Channel steamer. I caught a quick view of these sheets of thick paper untidily strewing the sea, not realizing that they were my novel for some time.

Then for six or seven years I wrote nothing. But that did not stop my habit of thinking. My husband and I had a small house built on the top of a hill in Yorkshire, where there was a forty-mile view from the windows. I hadn't very much to do, and I used to look out of the windows a lot at the clouds, and wish that I had half a dozen children. It was no use wishing. I hadn't. I swopped an old gramophone for a typewriter—it was, I remember, a Salter Standard—the letters of which were both broken and invisible. It was a heavy thing, but I lugged it around with me, and learned to type on it.

One day in '26 or '27, I am not sure of the year, I suddenly wrote a story straight through from beginning to end. I was absolutely amazed. I called it " Sultan Jekker." It was the first story I had written for a dozen years. At the age of fifteen I had written imitation Jack London, imitation Bret Harte, imitation anybody-who-took-my-fancy stories, and had them in an amateur magazine that used to be sent to my father's place to bind. But " Sultan Jekker " was not an imitation. It was mine. I wrote it straight on to the Salter typewriter, not stopping to look at the words, which I couldn't have seen anyway.

Well, my first story was written. I showed it to my husband, and he was surprised too. We wondered what to do with it. We had not

194

seen any of the same sort in popular magazines. But I found a different kind of magazine in the public library. It was called the *Adelphi*. I admired every contributor to this paper. There was a man called D. H. Lawrence, who had written two books that I had read—*Sons and Lovers*, and *Aaron's Rod*. I knew that he knew what he was talking about. He was the best contributor of all, I thought. And I thought, "Very well, then. Go where the best is, or nowhere at all."

All the same, I kept that story for a long time. I took it with me on a visit to London, meaning to drop it in the letter box of the *Adelphi*, which was then in Cursitor Street, Chancery Lane. I prowled about Chancery Lane every day for a week, never getting up enough courage to put it in the letter box. I took it back home with me.

Then one day I put the story into a clean envelope, enclosed a stamped envelope for return—nothing else, not a single word of writing—addressed it very simply to the editor of the *Adelphi*, and posted it. There was an uphill walk of a mile from the post box. I went back up the hill feeling as if I had committed a kind of crime. My husband tried to console me. " They can't do anything worse than send it back."

On the last day of March, 1927, I got a letter. At that time I had very few correspondents, and a letter was an event. But this was in my own handwriting ; I knew what it was, and did not want to open it. Of course I did open it eventually, and of course it contained my MS. There was also a note from John Middleton Murry, in his own handwriting. " Dear Sir," it ran, " this is a *good* story. Unfortunately, in all human probability the *Adelphi* will be coming to an end after two more numbers, and I am therefore unable to accept it. If, however, you still find the *Adelphi* being published after June next, send your story to me again."

I believe I could have walked straight off the cliff at the end of the garden, across to the moor top at the other side of the valley without going anywhere near the ground. Such was the effect of these words on me.

I waited to see if the *Adelphi* came out in September. But all the meantime I was writing away like one possessed. I wrote story after story in a trance. Very often they were badly worded. I was unable to get them right. Many of the stories in my first book I re-wrote from ten to fifteen times. "Frost in April" I typed out eighteen times. Quite boldly I sent a tale to a weekly called the *Outlook*. It was taken and printed, and paid for, too, but I hardly noticed it, so hungrily was I waiting for the *Adelphi* to reappear.

In the September it did come out again, and within eighteen months at least five of my stories had appeared in the *Adelphi*—there and nowhere else. I don't believe I sent them anywhere else. I had no other desire than to be with this rich company of writers.

At that time Mr. John W. Coulter was assistant editor. He was the first writing man I had ever met, and I thought he was half a god. I went with my husband to that office in Cursitor Street, and Mr. Coulter thought that my husband was the writer, and talked to him all the time. We were on our way to Spain, and had our luggage with us. My husband is, above all, a business man, and knows more about the structure of cloth than about books. He was getting in a literary fog, saying yes and no in the wrong places, when I jumped up and said miserably, "Look here, I wrote those stories." I can still see Mr. Coulter, looking like a schoolmaster behind a desk, with the two of us sitting in front of him like a couple of Will Hay's scholars.

On our return, Mr. Murry wrote to say that if I had enough stories for a volume he would do his best, though he could not promise anything, to help me place them with some publisher.

There it was. I didn't have to ask anybody for a thing. It just happened.

One day in March 1929 I went up to meet Mr. Murry himself. There was to be a luncheon at some restaurant, and I was asked to go. I was much too frightened to go. I was not used to eating in front of strangers, and did not want to choke. So I went merely to have coffee.

The place was up some stairs. There seemed to be a lot of people, but I only remember Mr. Murry, Mr. Coulter, Sir Richard Rees, and Dr. James Young. I asked the latter if he was *the* Dr. Jung, and he said no, a little coldly. My hands trembled so much that I could not lift my coffee-cup. Somebody—I believe it was Dr. Young—made me take some wine, and I had alternate drinks of coffee and wine until I came round. They have told me since that they were all much more scared than I was, and I can believe it now.

When I had been there a few minutes I handed my bundle of MSS. to Mr. Murry, saying briefly, " I've brought these." He had a case, and I had not. He put them in this case, oh so casually, and I hoped he would look after them, as I had not a whole copy of any story ; but I am sure that, if he had lost them, I should have been able to write them all again by heart.

However, he kept them most carefully, and sent them to Mr. Jonathan Cape. At his place they were read by Mr. Edward Garnett, who wrote and told me that he, too, liked them. The next thing that happened to me was the signing of an agreement, and, a month or two after that, the arrival of some proofs. By now I was getting used to amazing things. On October 14, 1929, out came my first volume of stories, *Frost in April*. And then, for weeks, nothing else happened.

My first reviewer was Humbert Wolfe. He was taking Gerald Gould's page in the *Sunday Observer*, while Mr. Gould was on holiday. Mr. Wolfe was not sure. He sniffed gingerly round my stories. I do not remember his exact words, but he said of one of them that it was " like a piece of fog cut out and preserved." I was genuinely pleased with such unique criticism.

Then the late Mr. Arnold Bennett gave me half a column in the *Evening Standard*, and for a week or two my name seemed to be in every paper I picked up. I was surprised to discover that I was a printed genius. There was only one dissentient voice. Somebody in the north of Ireland sneered at " this boy's lemonade masquerading as man's wine." Nearly everybody called me " he " because of my biblical name.

Now there are four volumes with my name on the cover. If Mr. Murry had not troubled to write to me about that first story, I should have gone on writing, because I could not have helped it. I might have returned to my childish habit of burning everything. Then there might have been a little less work for printers, binders, booksellers ; a little less wearying of eyesight, and tongue, and brain. But none of us would have been any wiser, or any more ignorant, than we are now.

PRINTED IN GREAT BRITAIN AT
THE PRESS OF THE PUBLISHERS